Communications in Computer and Information Science 2796

Series Editors

Rationale

The CCIS series is devoted to the publication of proceedings of computer science conferences. Its aim is to efficiently disseminate original research results in informatics in printed and electronic form. While the focus is on publication of peer-reviewed full papers presenting mature work, inclusion of reviewed short papers reporting on work in progress is welcome, too. Besides globally relevant meetings with internationally representative program committees guaranteeing a strict peer-reviewing and paper selection process, conferences run by societies or of high regional or national relevance are also considered for publication.

Topics

The topical scope of CCIS spans the entire spectrum of informatics ranging from foundational topics in the theory of computing to information and communications science and technology and a broad variety of interdisciplinary application fields.

Information for Volume Editors and Authors

Publication in CCIS is free of charge. No royalties are paid, however, we offer registered conference participants temporary free access to the online version of the conference proceedings on SpringerLink (http://link.springer.com) by means of an http referrer from the conference website and/or a number of complimentary printed copies, as specified in the official acceptance email of the event.

CCIS proceedings can be published in time for distribution at conferences or as post-proceedings, and delivered in the form of printed books and/or electronically as USBs and/or e-content licenses for accessing proceedings at SpringerLink. Furthermore, CCIS proceedings are included in the CCIS electronic book series hosted in the SpringerLink digital library at http://link.springer.com/bookseries/7899. Conferences publishing in CCIS are allowed to use our online conference service (Meteor) for managing the whole proceedings lifecycle (from submission and reviewing to preparing for publication) free of charge.

Publication process

The language of publication is exclusively English. Authors publishing in CCIS have to sign the Springer CCIS copyright transfer form, however, they are free to use their material published in CCIS for substantially changed, more elaborate subsequent publications elsewhere. For the preparation of the camera-ready papers/files, authors have to strictly adhere to the Springer CCIS Authors' Instructions and are strongly encouraged to use the CCIS LaTeX style files or templates.

Abstracting/Indexing

CCIS is abstracted/indexed in DBLP, Google Scholar, EI-Compendex, Mathematical Reviews, SCImago, Scopus. CCIS volumes are also submitted for the inclusion in ISI Proceedings.

How to start

To start the evaluation of your proposal for inclusion in the CCIS series, please send an e-mail to ccis@springer.com

Abraham Bagherjeiran · Nemanja Djuric ·
Kuang-chih Lee · Linsey Pang ·
Vladan Radosavljevic · Suju Rajan
Editors

Computational Advertising

19th International Workshop, AdKDD 2025
Toronto, ON, Canada, August 4, 2025
Proceedings

Springer

Editors
Abraham Bagherjeiran
ebay
San Jose, CA, USA

Nemanja Djuric
Aurora Innovation
Pittsburgh, PA, USA

Kuang-chih Lee
Walmart
Sunnyvale, CA, USA

Linsey Pang
Paypal
San Francisco, CA, USA

Vladan Radosavljevic
Spotify
New York, NY, USA

Suju Rajan
Amazon
Palo Alto, CA, USA

ISSN 1865-0929 ISSN 1865-0937 (electronic)
Communications in Computer and Information Science
ISBN 978-3-032-16357-8 ISBN 978-3-032-16358-5 (eBook)
https://doi.org/10.1007/978-3-032-16358-5

This Springer imprint is published by the registered company Springer Nature Switzerland AG
The registered company address is: Gewerbestrasse 11, 6330 Cham, Switzerland

Preface

The digital advertising field has always had challenging Machine Learning (ML) problems, learning from petabytes of data that is highly imbalanced, reactivity times in the milliseconds, and more recently compounded with the complex user's path to purchase across devices, across platforms, and even online/real-world behavior. The AdKDD workshop continues to be a forum for researchers in advertising, during and after the KDD conference where it is hosted. The 2025 edition was particularly timely because of the increasing application of Graph-based Neural Networks and Generative AI models in advertising. Coupled with privacy-preserving initiatives, such as those enforced by the EU General Data Protection Regulation (GDPR) or the California Consumer Privacy Act of 2018 (CCPA), the future of computational advertising is at an interesting crossroads. For this edition, we solicited papers that span the spectrum of deep user understanding while remaining privacy-preserving. In addition, we sought papers that discuss fairness in the context of advertising, to what extent hyper-personalization works, and whether the ad industry as a whole needs to think through more effective business models such as incrementality. We have always hosted several academic and industry luminaries as keynote speakers and have found our invited speaker series hosting expert practitioners to be an audience favorite. This year we continued with this practice and fielded a diverse set of keynote speakers and invited talks. As with past editions, we hoped to motivate researchers in this space to think not only about the ML aspects but also to spark conversations about the societal impact of online advertising.

As of the second quarter of 2024, the worldwide internet user spent more than 6.5 hours daily across all devices interacting with online content almost entirely sponsored by advertisements. At almost $700B global market size in 2024, and expected to reach $870B by 2027, digital advertising has already surpassed traditional ads in global spending and continues to grow. Digital advertising and in particular computational advertising is perhaps the most visible and ubiquitous application of machine learning and one that interacts directly with consumers. When done right, ads connect us to opportunities to enrich our lives, and when done badly they creep us out. Recently at the forefront of political battles between governments, large multinational corporations, and consumers, digital advertising remains a dynamic industry and research area.

Looking at the published literature over the last few years, many researchers might consider computational advertising a mature field. Yet, the opposite is true. Computational advertising is evolving from simple rule-based ads controlled by monolithic publishers and randomly rotating banner ads to highly personalized content experiences within native, video, and display formats on mobile devices, connected TV, and audio – all utilizing data amassed from petabytes of stored user data collected increasingly through inferred-identity providers. The increasing use of sequence models and the rise of Generative AI are spawning new directions, such as the auto-generation of ad creatives or pay-for-use shopping assistants. Ads are far from done.

There have been a total of nineteen AdKDD and TargetAd workshops to date, organized every year since 2007, which focused on highlighting state-of-the-art advances in computational advertising. The AdKDD workshops held in conjunction with KDD conferences in the past years (2017-2025) continue to generate interest from academia and industry as one of the top venues specifically for advertising research. We believe this is a unique forum for folks interested in aspects of digital advertising to get together, exchange notes, and get a pulse for the state of the art, especially in the industry.

The 2025 edition of the AdKDD workshop was held on August 4th, 2025 in Toronto, Canada, organized in conjuction with the KDD 2025 conference. Following the KDD tradition, reviews were single-blind with author names and affiliations listed. Submitted papers were assessed based on their novelty, technical quality, potential impact, insightfulness, depth, clarity, and reproducibility, with each paper receiving at least three independent reviews. There was a total of 17 full-paper submissions, with 10 papers accepted for presentation at the workshop and publication in the proceedings. For contributions co-authored by any committee members, these were objectively handled during the review phase by ensuring that none of the reviewers had a conflict of interest with regards to their assigned papers that they reviewed.

September 2025

Abraham Bagherjeiran
Nemanja Djuric
Kuang-chih Lee
Linsey Pang
Vladan Radosavljevic
Suju Rajan

Organization

Program Committee Chairs

Abraham Bagherjeiran	eBay, USA
Nemanja Djuric	Aurora Innovation, USA
Kuang-chih Lee	Walmart, USA
Linsey Pang	Salesforce, USA
Vladan Radosavljevic	Spotify, USA
Suju Rajan	Amazon, USA

Program Committe

Joel Barajas	Amazon, USA
Karla Caballero	University of California Santa Cruz, USA
Sudeep Fadadu	Aurora Innovation, USA
Djordje Gligorijevic	eBay, USA
Surender Kumar	Flipkart, India
Wei-Hsiang Lin	Spotify, USA
Qiang Ma	Amazon, USA
Poulami Maitra	Walmart, USA
Andreas Merentitis	OLX Group, Germany
Shaunak Mishra	Amazon, USA
Sri Sri Perangur	Netflix, USA
Wen Pu	LinkedIn, USA
Shang Shang	Amazon, USA
Talha Ahmad Siddiqui	Aurora Innovation, USA
Fabrizio Silvestri	Sapienza University of Rome, Italy
Lampros Stavrogiannis	Aristotle University of Thessaloniki, Greece
Moussa Taifi	Xandr, USA
Yana Volkovich	Xandr, USA
Weiru Zhang	Alibaba, China

Contents

Hierarchical Group-Wise Ranking Framework for Recommendation Models 1
YaChen Yan, Liubo Li, and Ravi Choudhary

A Bayesian-DLM-CF Framework for Real-Time Display Advertising 15
Michael Els and David Banks

MTMD: A Multi-task Multi-domain Framework for Unified Ad Lightweight Ranking at Pinterest 29
Xiao Yang, Peifeng Yin, Abe Engle, Jinfeng Zhuang, and Ling Leng

Mitigating Position Bias in Click Predictor Models: A Novel Downsampling Approach for Enhanced Accuracy and Efficiency 42
Phuong Ha Nguyen, Djordje Gligorijevic, Hung Nguyen, Sheng Shen, Zhenke Xi, and Abraham Bagherjeiran

SIDE: Semantic ID Embedding for Effective Learning from Sequences 57
Dinesh Ramasamy, Shakti Kumar, Chris Cadonic, Jiaxin Yang, Sohini Roychowdhury, Esam Abdel Rhman, and Srihari Reddy

Profit Aware Ad Ranking with Relevance Constraint 71
Manavender Malgireddy, Dongyue Xie, Sergey Kolbin, Kurt Zimmer, Masoum Mosmer, and Patrick Phelps

More Ads, Happier Shoppers: Unified-Valuation Ad Allocation at Scale 85
Sergey Kolbin, Arushi Jain, Manavender Malgireddy, Kurt Zimmer, Masoum Mosmer, and Patrick Phelps

DCN^2: Interplay of *Implicit* Collision Weights and *Explicit* Cross Layers for Large-Scale Recommendation 99
Blaž Škrlj, Yonatan Karni, Grega Gašperšič, Blaž Mramor, Yulia Stolin, Martin Jakomin, Jasna Urbančič, Yuval Dishi, Natalia Silberstein, Ophir Friedler, and Assaf Klein

Click A, Buy B: Rethinking Conversion Attribution in E-Commerce Recommendations 113
Xiangyu Zeng, Amit Jaspal, Bin Liu, Goutham Panneeru, Kevin Huang, Nicolas Bievre, Mohit Jaggi, Prathap Maniraju, and Ankur Jain

Large Language Models for Detecting Gambling Advertisement Images to Enhance the Efficiency of the Creative Review Process 125
Edward L. Martis and Jayesh Santosh Asawa

Author Index 139

Hierarchical Group-Wise Ranking Framework for Recommendation Models

YaChen Yan(✉), Liubo Li, and Ravi Choudhary

Credit Karma, San Francisco, CA, USA
{yachen.yan,liubo.li,ravi.choudhary}@creditkarma.com

Abstract. In modern recommender systems, CTR/CVR models are increasingly trained with ranking objectives to improve item ranking quality. While this shift aligns training more closely with serving goals, most existing methods rely on in-batch negative sampling, which predominantly surfaces easy negatives. This limits the model's ability to capture fine-grained user preferences and weakens overall ranking performance. To address this, we propose a Hierarchical Group-wise Ranking Framework with two key components. First, we apply residual vector quantization to user embeddings to generate hierarchical user codes that partition users into hierarchical, trie-structured clusters. Second, we apply listwise ranking losses to user-item pairs at each level of the hierarchy, where shallow levels group loosely similar users and deeper levels group highly similar users, reinforcing learning-to-rank signals through progressively harder negatives. Since users with similar preferences and content exposure tend to yield more informative negatives, applying ranking losses within these hierarchical user groups serves as an effective approximation of hard negative mining. Our approach improves ranking performance without requiring complex real-time context collection or retrieval infrastructure. Extensive experiments demonstrate that the proposed framework consistently enhances both model calibration and ranking accuracy, offering a scalable and practical solution for industrial recommender systems.

Keywords: Recommender Systems · Learning to Rank · Vector Quantization

1 Introduction

Click-through rate (CTR) and conversion rate (CVR) prediction models play a pivotal role in large-scale recommender systems and online advertising. While most modern systems rely on binary classification objectives such as log loss to estimate the likelihood of user actions, enhancing the ranking quality of model predictions has become a critical direction for improving user experience and achieving business goals. In this context, learning-to-rank (LTR) objectives, including pairwise and listwise losses, are widely adopted to better capture users' relative preferences among items.

A. Bagherjeiran et al. (Eds.): AdKDD 2025, CCIS 2796, pp. 1–14, 2026.
https://doi.org/10.1007/978-3-032-16358-5_1

However, a persistent challenge lies in constructing meaningful item comparisons during training. In particular, existing ranking losses often rely on in-batch negative sampling or uniformly sampled negative pairs, which tend to overemphasize easy negatives while underutilizing more informative, harder negatives. Recent research has shown that sampling negatives based on similarity or gradient-based importance can significantly improve model performance, but often at the cost of increased computational overhead, particularly in real-time environments. Existing context-aware approaches such as JRC [5] and SBCR [9] improve ranking performance by leveraging online ranked list logging. However, these methods require real-time infrastructure and tightly integrated systems, which increases deployment complexity and limits scalability in production environments. Furthermore, CVR models often suffer from sparse in-session user feedback, limiting the effectiveness of context-aware negative sampling based on in-session interactions.

To address these challenges, we propose a novel **Hierarchical Group-wise Ranking Framework** that improves ranking performance without relying on real-time context or nearest-neighbor retrieval. Our approach uses residual vector quantization (RVQ) to learn hierarchical user codes and group user-item pairs into multi-level clusters. Within each group, we apply listwise ranking losses over progressively harder negatives, based on the intuition that users with similar profiles or behaviors yield more informative comparisons. This hierarchical, multi-resolution cross-user sampling provides an efficient and scalable alternative for industrial recommendation systems. The main contributions of this paper can be summarized as follows:

- We propose a residual vector quantization module to encode user embeddings into hierarchical discrete codes, which serve as the foundation for multi-level user grouping. This structure enables dynamic and granular control over the difficulty level of sampled negatives during training.
- We introduce a hierarchical group-wise listwise ranking loss that applies ranking loss within user groups defined at each hierarchical level. By varying the granularity level of grouping, our method progressively surfaces harder negatives, offering an efficient alternative to gradient-based sampling strategies.
- We integrate this hierarchical ranking objective with standard calibration losses in a multi-task learning framework and demonstrate that our method improves both convergence efficiency and ranking performance across multiple domains, without requiring real-time context collection or retrieval infrastructure. Our framework serves as a plug-in component that introduces negligible additional training overhead and zero serving latency.

2 Preliminaries

The recommendation model with binary relevance is commonly formulated as a binary classification problem optimized with binary logistic loss. The binary logistic loss function is defined as:

$$\mathcal{L}_{\text{logloss}} = -\frac{1}{N}\sum_{i=1}^{N}[y_i \log(\hat{y}_i) + (1 - y_i)\log(1 - \hat{y}_i)] \tag{1}$$

where $\hat{y}_i$ represents the predicted probability and $y_i \in \{0, 1\}$ is the binary feedback label. To enhance ranking performance, recent approaches incorporate Learning-to-Rank (LTR) losses as auxiliary objectives. The combined objective function $\mathcal{L} = \mathcal{L}_{\text{logloss}} + \lambda\mathcal{L}_{rank}$ integrates binary logistic loss with either pairwise ranking loss (comparing item pairs) or listwise ranking loss (optimizing the entire item list ordering), where λ controls the contribution of the ranking component. In this setting, the ranking loss typically operates on the model's predicted scores over user-item pairs. Negative samples for the ranking loss are commonly drawn uniformly from other user-item pairs within the same training batch (i.e., in-batch negative sampling) to construct contrastive comparisons during training.

Without loss of generality, the notation used throughout this paper for recommendation models with binary relevance is as follows: the training dataset consists of instances (x_u, x_i, y), where x_u and x_i denote user and item features respectively, $y \in \{0, 1\}$ indicates the binary user-item feedback label. The raw user features x_u and item features x_i are processed by their respective networks to obtain user embedding $\mathbf{e}_u$ and item embedding $\mathbf{e}_i$. These embeddings are then fed into a main network that outputs logit s, which is transformed into the predicted probability $\hat{y} = \sigma(s)$ using the sigmoid function σ. The primary optimization objective is the binary logistic loss comparing $\hat{y}$ against ground truth labels y, while a ranking loss encourages correct ordering of items. This general notation serves as the foundation for our proposed model as well, which extends these concepts with additional specialized notation to capture our proposed framework.

3 Negative Sampling Challenges and Theoretical Gradient Analysis

While widely adopted, CTR/CVR models that combine binary logistic and ranking losses still face key optimization challenges—namely, inefficient negative sampling and slow convergence. Existing methods often focus on easy negatives that offer limited learning value. Through gradient-based analysis, we show that sampling harder negatives in proportion to their gradient norms significantly improves convergence. This insight motivates our hierarchical group-wise sampling strategy, which efficiently surfaces challenging negatives from similar users during training.

3.1 Limitations of Uniform Sampling

Traditional negative sampling strategies, such as uniform in-batch sampling, often prioritize easy negatives that are trivial for the model to distinguish. This limits the model's ability to learn fine-grained user preference signals and ultimately undermines ranking performance. To address this, recent work has explored retrieving harder negatives via approximate nearest neighbor (ANN) search [7], which improves the model's capacity to capture subtle distinctions. However, ANN-based methods introduce significant computational overhead and are generally better suited to retrieval models than to ranking models, which require capturing complex user-item interactions beyond inner products and supporting online learning. The key challenge is to efficiently surface informative hard negatives during training, without relying on real-time context collection or exhaustive nearest-neighbor search.

3.2 Gradient-Based Sampling Theory

Consider a training batch with positive and negative samples. An importance-weighted stochastic gradient descent (SGD) update for the ranking loss can be expressed as:

$$\theta_{t+1} = \theta_t - \eta \frac{1}{Np^-} \nabla_{\theta_t} l(s^+, s^-) \tag{2}$$

where η is the learning rate. θ_t represents the parameters at iteration t, θ_{t+1} the updated parameters. p^- denotes the probability of selecting a particular negative instance (x_u, x_i, y^-). The scaling factor $\frac{1}{Np^-}$ ensures an unbiased gradient estimate. Following derivations in variance reduction [3][?], let $g = \frac{1}{Np^-} \nabla_{\theta_t} l(s^+, s^-)$ be the weighted gradient, we can write the convergence rate as:

$$\begin{aligned} E\Delta_t &= \|\theta_t - \theta^*\|^2 - E_{P^-}(\|\theta_{t+1} - \theta^*\|^2) \\ &= 2\eta E_{P^-}(g)^T(\theta_t - \theta^*) - \eta^2 E_{P^-}(g)^T E_{P^-}(g) \\ &\quad - \eta^2 \mathrm{Tr}(V_{P^-}(g)) \end{aligned} \tag{3}$$

where P^- is the negative sampling distribution for a given positive example (x_u, x_i, y^+). This formulation shows that convergence can be improved by selecting negative examples from a distribution that reduces $\mathrm{Tr}(V_{P^-}(g))$, which quantifies the total gradient variance introduced by the negative sampling. The optimal sampling strategy is

$$p^{*-} = \arg\min_{p^-} \mathrm{Tr}(V_{P^-}(g)) \propto \|\nabla_{\theta_t} l(s^+, s^-)\|^2 \tag{4}$$

The above analysis shows that the optimal negative sampling distribution is proportional to the squared gradient norm of each instance, favoring samples that contribute larger updates to the model. This approach is particularly valuable in recommendation systems, where the vast majority of negative examples contribute minimal learning signals. Prioritizing hard negatives with large gradient contributions reduces the variance of gradient estimates and accelerates convergence, aligning with established variance reduction principles in stochastic optimization and motivating our gradient-informed sampling strategy.

4 Proposed Framework

To operationalize the above theoretical insight, we propose a hierarchical group-wise negative sampling strategy that approximates the optimal distribution without incurring costly computations. Our approach clusters users based on profile or behavioral similarity, and groups the associated user-item samples according to these user clusters across multiple hierarchical levels. This structure enables the model to sample negatives from users of varying similarity: from coarse groups capturing general behavior patterns to fine-grained subgroups reflecting closely shared interests. Intuitively, negatives samples drawn from similar users are more informative, as similar users tend to be exposed to overlapping content and exhibit comparable preferences. By leveraging negative samples from similar users, our method introduces progressively harder negatives that enhance the learning signal throughout the hierarchy. This promotes more effective optimization of ranking loss while maintaining computational efficiency, ultimately improving learning dynamics in CTR/CVR prediction tasks.

We designed the proposed framework, as illustrated in Fig. 1 with three main components:

Hierarchical User Code Generation: We quantize each user embedding into a structured sequence of discrete codes using multi-stage residual vector quantization, where each stage uses a codebook to quantize the remaining error from the previous level. This produces a hierarchical code sequence that forms a trie-like structure, where higher levels represent broad semantic groupings and deeper levels capture fine-grained user distinctions.

Hierarchical Group-wise Ranking Objective: Based on the generated user codes, we organize users into nested groups where users sharing the same prefix codes at each level are grouped together, forming a trie-like structure of increasing similarity. We apply listwise ranking loss within each group, computing the loss over groups containing user-item pairs with shared code prefixes. By varying the group depth, we control negative difficulty: shallow levels provide easier negatives from loosely similar users, while deeper levels yield harder negatives from highly similar users. To balance contributions across hierarchy levels, we employ an uncertainty-based weighting scheme, enabling the model to adaptively focus on the most informative hierarchy depths during training.

Multi-objective Training Strategy: Our training objective combines three components: a primary calibration loss on predictions from the original user embedding, an auxiliary calibration loss on predictions from the quantized embedding (using straight-through estimator to enable gradient flow), and the proposed hierarchical ranking loss. Unlike traditional vector quantization approaches, we omit commitment loss to preserve adaptability in dynamic recommendation settings, instead relying on the auxiliary calibration loss to encourage alignment between original and quantized embeddings while maintaining flexibility for evolving user preferences and behaviors.

In our model specifically, the user embedding $\mathbf{e}_u$ undergoes residual vector quantization to produce the quantized user embedding $\mathbf{e}_u^q$ and user hierarchical

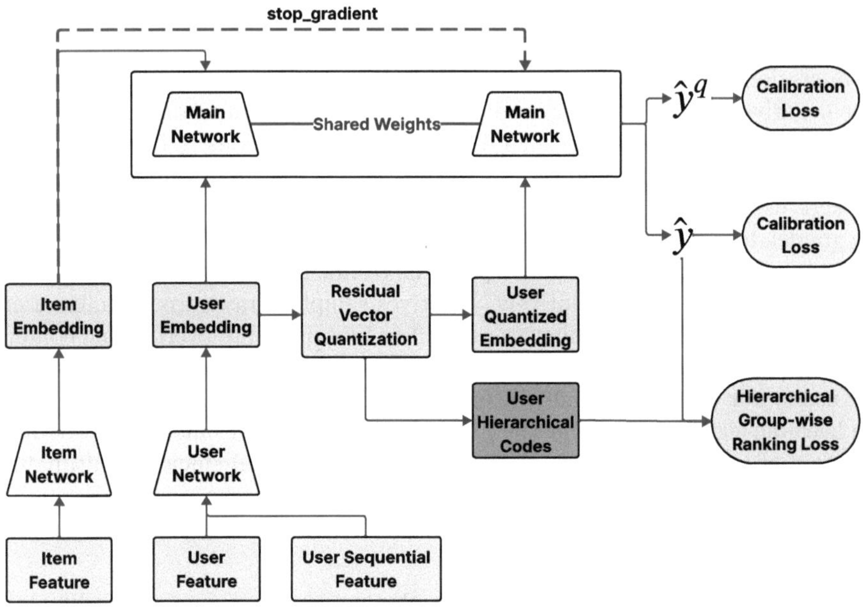

Fig. 1. The Architecture of the Proposed Framework

codes $\mathbf{c}_u$. When the shared main network uses the quantized user embedding $\mathbf{e}_u^q$ and the item embedding $\mathbf{e}_i$ as inputs, it produces logit s^q and the corresponding predicted probability $\hat{y}^q = \sigma(s^q)$. To avoid conflicting gradients between the dual prediction paths, we stop the gradient flow from the auxiliary loss into the item embedding by applying stop_gradient($\mathbf{e}_i$) when computing $\hat{y}^q$. This ensures that only the user network receives updates from the auxiliary calibration loss, preserving training stability. Both the original and quantized predictions ($\hat{y}$ and $\hat{y}^q$) are optimized using calibration loss against ground truth labels. Additionally, the user hierarchical codes $\mathbf{c}_u$ are used to compute a hierarchical group-wise ranking loss to further enhance ranking performance. These notations ($\mathbf{e}_u^q$, $\mathbf{c}_u$, s^q, $\hat{y}^q$) extend the general framework presented earlier and are specific to our quantization-based approach, introducing additional variables necessary to describe our model's unique architecture and optimization strategy.

4.1 Hierarchical User Codes Generation

To capture structured user similarity and enable efficient group-wise sampling, we discretize user embeddings using a residual vector quantization (RVQ) framework. This process encodes each user into a sequence of discrete codes, referred to as hierarchical user codes, which form the foundation of our multi-resolution user grouping strategy. Figure 2 illustrates the cascaded quantization process and the resulting hierarchical user code structure.

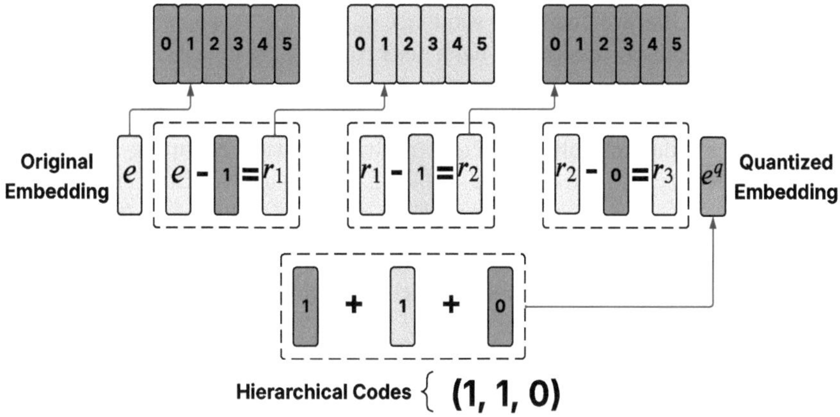

Fig. 2. Residual Vector Quantization

Given a user embedding $\mathbf{e}_u \in \mathbb{R}^d$ produced by the user network (which may include contextual or sequential features), we apply an L-stage residual quantization procedure to obtain a code sequence $\mathbf{c}_u = [\mathbf{c}_{u,1}, \ldots, \mathbf{c}_{u,L}]$. At each stage l, a codebook $\mathcal{C}^{(l)} = \{\mathcal{C}_1^{(l)}, \ldots, \mathcal{C}_K^{(l)}\}$ is used to quantize the residual vector passed down from the previous level. These codebooks are arranged in a cascaded structure, where each level incrementally refines the remaining quantization error:

$$\begin{aligned} \mathbf{r}_u^{(1)} &= \mathbf{e}_u \\ \mathbf{c}_{u,l} &= \arg\min_k \|\mathbf{r}_u^{(l)} - \mathcal{C}_k^{(l)}\|_2^2 \\ \mathbf{r}_u^{(l+1)} &= \mathbf{r}_u^{(l)} - \mathcal{C}_{\mathbf{c}_{u,l}}^{(l)} \end{aligned} \tag{5}$$

The quantized embedding is reconstructed by summing codebook vectors from all stages:

$$\hat{\mathbf{e}}_u = \sum_{l=1}^{L} \mathcal{C}_{\mathbf{c}_{u,l}}^{(l)} \tag{6}$$

To ensure stable learning and effective usage of codebook entries, each codebook is updated using Exponential Moving Average (EMA) strategy. Following each assignment, usage statistics and accumulated residuals are used to softly update the code vectors:

$$\mathcal{C}_k^{(l)} \leftarrow m \cdot \mathcal{C}_k^{(l)} + (1-m) \cdot \mu_k, \quad N_k \leftarrow m \cdot N_k + (1-m) \cdot n_k \tag{7}$$

where μ_k and n_k represent the average and count of residuals assigned to code k, and m is the EMA decay rate. We also apply Laplace smoothing to the EMA count to avoid instability from rare updates. To prevent representation collapse, we replace infrequently used codes with randomly sampled embeddings from the current batch, following SoundStream [8].

The resulting hierarchical code sequence $\mathbf{c}_u = [\mathbf{c}_{u,1}, \ldots, \mathbf{c}_{u,L}]$ defines a multi-level grouping scheme, assigning each user to a path in a trie-like structure. Higher levels represent coarse semantic groupings, while deeper levels capture increasingly fine-grained distinctions. Users sharing longer prefix codes are considered more similar, enabling efficient multi-resolution grouping where upper levels offer diversity and lower levels surface harder negatives from closely related users.

4.2 Hierarchical Group-Wise Ranking Objective

The hierarchical user codes $\mathbf{c}_u = [\mathbf{c}_{u,1}, \ldots, \mathbf{c}_{u,L}]$ enable structured negative sampling through multi-level user grouping. At each level l, users sharing the same prefix $(\mathbf{c}_{u,1}, \ldots, \mathbf{c}_{u,l})$ form nested clusters of growing specificity. This structure defines semantically coherent user-item groups at multiple granularities, allowing listwise ranking losses to be applied within groups of progressively similar users—supporting harder negative sampling and more effective ranking supervision.

As illustrated in Fig. 3, we recursively partition user-item pairs into finer groups according to these hierarchical prefixes. Within each group, the users' positive items are treated as positive examples, while users' negative items serve as negatives. By varying the group depth l, we effectively control the difficulty of sampled negatives: shallower levels provide easier negatives from loosely similar users, while deeper levels yield harder negatives from highly similar users who share more behavioral or contextual overlap and content exposure.

To train the model on these grouped samples, we adopt the Regression Compatible Listwise Cross Entropy loss (ListCE) [1], which replaces the softmax transformation with the sigmoid function based normalization. This improves compatibility between ranking and calibration losses under binary relevance.

Let $G_1^{(l)}, G_2^{(l)}, \ldots, G_{M_l}^{(l)}$ denote the groups formed at level l, where each group $G_m^{(l)}$ contains user-item pairs sharing the same code prefix. The listwise loss at level l is defined as:

$$\mathcal{L}_{\text{listce}}^{(l)}(s, y) = \frac{1}{M_l} \sum_{m=1}^{M_l} \sum_{i \in G_m^{(l)}} -\tilde{y}_i^{(l,m)} \log \left(\frac{\sigma(s_i)}{\sum_{j \in G_m^{(l)}} \sigma(s_j)} \right) \tag{8}$$

where s_i is the predicted logit for user-item pair i, and $\sigma(s_i)$ represents its sigmoid-transformed score. The corresponding normalized label $\tilde{y}_i^{(l,m)}$ is computed as: $\tilde{y}_i^{(l,m)} = \frac{y_i}{\sum_{j \in G_m^{(l)}} y_j + \epsilon}$, ensuring that labels are normalized within each group $G_m^{(l)}$.

To balance the contribution from different hierarchy levels, we introduce an uncertainty-based weighting scheme [4]. Each level l is associated with a learnable uncertainty parameter σ_l. The total hierarchical ranking loss is defined as:

$$\mathcal{L}_{\text{hierarchical}} = \sum_{l=1}^{L} \left(\frac{1}{2\sigma_l^2} \mathcal{L}_{\text{listwise}}^{(l)}(s, y) + \log \sigma_l \right) \tag{9}$$

This formulation enables the model to adaptively weight ranking loss from each level based on its estimated uncertainty. As a result, the model learns to focus on the most informative hierarchy depths during training, while preserving stable and balanced optimization across levels.

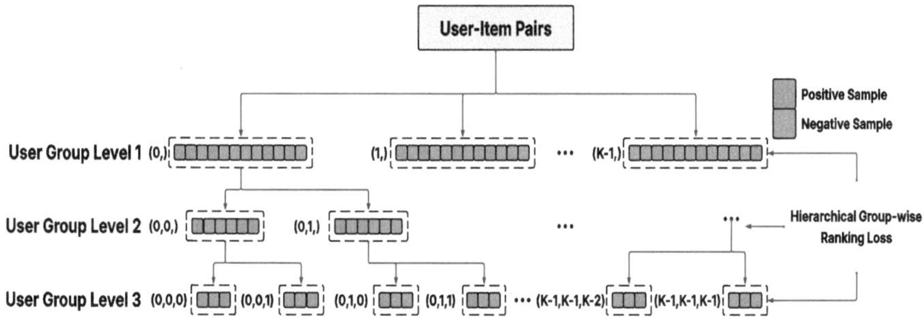

Fig. 3. Hierarchical Group-wise Ranking Framework. A trie-structured approach organizes user-item pairs into multi-level user groups based on shared code prefixes. Positive (red) and negative (blue) examples are drawn within each group to supervise ranking objectives. Varying the group depth enables learning to rank over increasingly fine-grained user similarity. (Color figure online)

4.3 Multi-objective Training Strategy

Objective Function Formulation. Our overall training objective integrates three components: a primary calibration loss on the predicted click-through probability from the original user embedding, a secondary calibration loss from the quantized user embedding, and a hierarchical group-wise listwise ranking loss. Formally, the total loss is defined as:

$$\begin{aligned}\mathcal{L}_{\text{loss}} &= \mathcal{L}_{\text{logloss}}(\hat{y}, y) \\ &+ \lambda \mathcal{L}_{\text{logloss}}(\hat{y}^q, y) \\ &+ \mathcal{L}_{\text{hierarchical}}\end{aligned} \tag{10}$$

The first term, $\mathcal{L}_{\text{logloss}}(\hat{y}, y)$, serves as the primary loss for calibrating the model's click-through probability prediction using the original user embedding $\mathbf{e}_u$. This component ensures that the model produces well-calibrated probability estimates suitable for real-world serving, ensuring compatibility with recommendation systems that consume predicted probabilities.

The second term, $\mathcal{L}_{\text{logloss}}(\hat{y}^q, y)$, introduces an auxiliary calibration loss applied to predictions derived from the quantized user embedding $\mathbf{e}_u^q$, obtained via residual vector quantization. Importantly, to enable backpropagation through the non-differentiable quantization operation, we apply a straight-through estimator (STE):

$$\mathbf{e}_u^q = \mathbf{e}_u + \text{stop\_gradient}(\hat{\mathbf{e}}_u - \mathbf{e}_u) \tag{11}$$

Here, $\hat{\mathbf{e}}_u = \sum_{l=1}^{L} \mathcal{C}_{\mathbf{c}_{u,l}}^{(l)}$ represents the quantized embedding. This formulation makes $\mathbf{e}_u^q$ match $\hat{\mathbf{e}}_u$ in the forward pass, while gradients flow through $\mathbf{e}_u$ in the backward pass, enabling user encoder training with quantization-based regularization.

Although $\mathbf{e}_u^q$ is not used during serving, this auxiliary loss regularizes the shared user network by encouraging it to produce embeddings that are not only predictive but also structurally compressible and cluster-aware. Specifically, it helps align the user embedding space with the quantized codebook space, promoting smoother transitions and more stable quantization behavior. This alignment facilitates better codebook utilization and supports dynamic clustering under shifting user distributions. As a result, it improves training stability by maintaining a semantically meaningful and adaptive latent structure.

The final component, $\mathcal{L}_{\text{hierarchical}}$, is the proposed hierarchical group-wise listwise ranking loss. It utilizes trie-structured user codes generated via residual vector quantization to group user-item pairs into semantically coherent user clusters at multiple levels of granularity. By applying the ranking loss within these groups, the model receives user cluster-aware ranking supervision using progressively harder negatives drawn from similar users. This structure improves ranking quality without incurring the cost of real-time context collection or explicit nearest-neighbor retrieval.

Clustering Adaptability. Traditional vector quantization frameworks such as VQ-VAE [6] typically employ a commitment loss (e.g., $\|\mathbf{e}_u - \hat{\mathbf{e}}_u\|^2$) to explicitly align the continuous embedding with its quantized counterpart. However, we omit this component in our framework due to the dynamic nature of real-time recommendation settings, where user embeddings must continually adapt to evolving preferences, behaviors, and contextual signals.

Enforcing a commitment loss would constrain user embeddings to remain near static quantized representations, limiting their ability to transition across clusters and adapt in response to new interactions. Instead, we allow the primary calibration loss $\mathcal{L}_{\text{logloss}}(\hat{y}, y)$ to guide representation learning, maintaining expressiveness and adaptability. To softly encourage alignment between the embedding and its quantized version, we incorporate an auxiliary calibration loss $\mathcal{L}_{\text{logloss}}(\hat{y}^q, y)$ applied to the quantized prediction. This auxiliary loss serves as a task-driven regularizer, encouraging meaningful and quantization-friendly embeddings without rigid constraints.

Our approach supports flexible and generalizable representation learning under streaming or non-stationary conditions, aligning with insights from recent work on real-time indexing [2], which similarly avoids commitment loss to preserve adaptability.

5 Experiments

In this section, we evaluate our framework on two large-scale public datasets, demonstrating that hierarchical group-wise ranking significantly improves model performance. During experiments, we focus on evaluating the effectiveness of our proposed models and answering the following questions.

- **Q1**: How does our proposed framework perform on ranking tasks? Is it effective and efficient in extremely high-dimensional and sparse data settings?
- **Q2**: How well does our framework handle user cold-start scenarios with limited interaction history? Can it maintain robust performance when user signals are sparse?

5.1 Experiment Setup

Datasets. We evaluate our proposed model using two publicly available real-world datasets commonly utilized in research: KuaiRand and Taobao. The data is randomly divided into three subsets: 70% for training, 10% for validation, and 20% for testing. We applied stratified sampling to ensure that each user has positive samples in every data subset.

- **KuaiRand**[1] is a recommendation dataset collected from the video-sharing mobile app Kuaishou.
- **Taobao**[2] is a Taobao E-commerce dataset released Alibaba.

Evaluation Metrics. For evaluating the ranking performance, we adopt LogLoss and AUC metric and further compute the Group AUC (GAUC) to measure the goodness of intra-user ranking ability. Group AUC calculates the AUC for each user and aggregates them using a weighted average based on the number of impressions, capturing per-user ranking quality and better reflecting real-world performance.

5.2 Model Performance Comparison (Q1)

The overall performance of different losses is listed in Table 1. We have the following observations in terms of objective function effectiveness:

- **LogLoss** serves as the baseline objective and yields the lowest performance across both datasets, demonstrating the limitations of using a pure calibration loss without ranking supervision.
- **LogLoss + PairwiseLogistic** and **LogLoss + SoftmaxCE** show consistent improvements over the baseline, highlighting the benefit of incorporating pairwise or listwise ranking losses into model training.

[1] https://kuairand.com/.
[2] https://tianchi.aliyun.com/dataset/649.

Table 1. Performance Comparison of Different Ranking Objectives on KuaiRand and Taobao Datasets.

Objective	KuaiRand			Taobao		
	LogLoss	AUC	GAUC	LogLoss	AUC	GAUC
LogLoss	0.5735	0.7510	0.6911	0.2011	0.6420	0.5708
LogLoss + PairwiseLogistic	0.5723	0.7524	0.6921	0.2002	0.6435	0.5728
LogLoss + SoftmaxCE	0.5727	0.7520	0.6920	0.2005	0.6428	0.5720
LogLoss + ListCE	0.5709	0.7537	0.6932	0.1995	0.6443	0.5734
JRC	0.5713	0.7533	0.6930	0.1993	0.6540	0.5732
GroupCE (proposed)	**0.5681**	**0.7556**	**0.6953**	**0.1982**	**0.6556**	**0.5745**

- **LogLoss + ListCE** and **JRC** achieve further gains, demonstrating that listwise ranking objectives with calibration-compatible designs lead to stronger overall performance.
- **GroupCE** achieves the best performance across all metrics. These results validate the effectiveness of our hierarchical group-wise ranking strategy, which enables progressively harder negative sampling through structured user clustering.

5.3 Cold Start Capability (Q2)

To assess the model's robustness in user cold-start scenarios, we evaluate its performance on user cohorts with limited interaction history. Since our model leverages hierarchical user codes for structured contrastive learning, we hypothesize that it can capture discriminative patterns at the cluster level, enabling it to maintain ranking quality even when individual user signals are sparse.

Table 2. Performance Comparison in Cold-Start Scenarios on KuaiRand Dataset.

Objective	KuaiRand (Cold)			KuaiRand (Warm)		
	LogLoss	AUC	GAUC	LogLoss	AUC	GAUC
LogLoss	0.6189	0.7298	0.6718	0.5683	0.7454	0.6945
LogLoss + PairwiseLogistic	0.6171	0.7305	0.6735	0.5670	0.7461	0.6955
LogLoss + SoftmaxCE	0.6175	0.7302	0.6730	0.5674	0.7458	0.6952
LogLoss + ListCE	0.6137	0.7308	0.6732	0.5662	0.7469	0.6962
JRC	0.6145	0.7308	0.6738	0.5664	0.7475	0.6968
GroupCE (proposed)	**0.6115**	**0.7320**	**0.6786**	**0.5636**	**0.7489**	**0.6986**

We stratify users by the number of impressions in the KuaiRand training set into cold (≤ 20) and warm ($20 - 50$) groups, and assess model performance on the corresponding users in the test set. As shown in Table 2, our proposed GroupCE framework consistently outperforms baselines across both user segments, with the most notable GAUC gains observed in the cold-start group. These results indicate that hierarchical clustering introduces effective user-level priors, enabling better ranking performance even with limited user history, a promising direction for addressing cold-start challenges in recommendation systems.

6 Conclusion

We propose a Hierarchical Group-wise Ranking Framework that enhances CTR/CVR model performance by leveraging residual vector quantization to construct hierarchical user clusters for structured, cluster-aware ranking supervision. By grouping user-item pairs into semantically coherent clusters, our framework enables efficient and effective hard negative sampling without requiring real-time context collection or incurring the computational overhead of cross-user retrieval. We introduce a hierarchical listwise ranking loss to model item ordering across varying levels of user similarity and complement it with calibration objectives applied to both original and quantized embeddings. Extensive experiments across multiple datasets demonstrate consistent improvements in both ranking accuracy and calibration quality, particularly under sparse user behavior scenarios. The proposed framework provides a scalable and generalizable solution for industrial recommendation systems and opens new directions for ranking optimization via quantization-based hierarchical clustering, enabling efficient learning-to-rank under limited user feedback.

References

1. Bai, A., et al.: Regression compatible listwise objectives for calibrated ranking with binary relevance. In: Proceedings of the 32nd ACM International Conference on Information and Knowledge Management, pp. 4502–4508 (2023)
2. Bin, X., et al.: Real-time indexing for large-scale recommendation by streaming vector quantization retriever. arXiv preprint arXiv:2501.08695 (2025)
3. Katharopoulos, A., Fleuret, F.: Not all samples are created equal: deep learning with importance sampling. In: International Conference on Machine Learning, pp. 2525–2534. PMLR (2018)
4. Kendall, A., Gal, Y., Cipolla, R.: Multi-task learning using uncertainty to weigh losses for scene geometry and semantics. In: Proceedings of the IEEE Conference on Computer Vision And Pattern Recognition, pp. 7482–7491 (2018)
5. Sheng, X.R., et al.: Joint optimization of ranking and calibration with contextualized hybrid model. In: Proceedings of the 29th ACM SIGKDD Conference on Knowledge Discovery and Data Mining, pp. 4813–4822 (2023)
6. Van Den Oord, A., Vinyals, O., et al.: Neural discrete representation learning. Adv. Neural Inf. Proc. Syst. **30** (2017)
7. Xiong, L., et al.: Approximate Nearest Neighbor Negative Contrastive Learning for Dense Text Retrieval. arXiv preprint arXiv:2007.00808 (2020)

8. Zeghidour, N., Luebs, A., Omran, A., Skoglund, J., Tagliasacchi, M.: Soundstream: an end-to-end neural audio codec. IEEE/ACM Trans. Audio, Speech, Lang. Proc. **30**, 495–507 (2021)
9. Zhang, S., Liu, H., Bao, W., Yu, E., Song, Y.: A self-boosted framework for calibrated ranking. In: Proceedings of the 30th ACM SIGKDD Conference on Knowledge Discovery and Data Mining, pp. 6226–6235 (2024)

A Bayesian-DLM-CF Framework for Real-Time Display Advertising

Michael Els[1(✉)] and David Banks[2]

[1] InMarket, Austin, TX 78701, USA
mels@inmarket.com
[2] Duke University, Durham, NC 27708, USA
banks@stat.duke.edu
https://inmarket.com, https://stat.duke.edu

Abstract. Click-through rate prediction underpins real-time bidding strategies in display advertising. We propose a unified approach that integrates beta-based Bayesian priors, Dynamic Linear Models, and collaborative filtering to address data sparsity, temporal dynamics, and neighbor relationships. A hierarchical Bayesian structure shares information across campaigns from the same advertiser, improving estimates when per-campaign data are limited. On a real-world dataset, our method outperforms baselines including standard collaborative filtering, random forest, and XGBoost, achieving superior log-loss and mean squared error.

Keywords: Real-Time Bidding · Click-Through Rate · Recommender Systems

1 Introduction

Predicting click-through rate (CTR) is a cornerstone of real-time bidding (RTB) systems in online advertising. Small improvements in prediction accuracy can significantly increase the success of ad campaigns, as advertisers and platforms seek to optimize both user engagement and revenue generation [10]. Despite the steady advance of machine learning methods for CTR, several challenges persist. First, human behavior exhibits considerable variation over time, leading to temporal shifts that degrade the performance of static models. Second, the sheer number of possible (person, item) pairs, combined with typically rare click data, creates serious data sparsity issues that can undermine a model's ability to generalize. Finally, real-time environments demand fast and reliable predictions at scale, placing practical constraints on the complexity and latency of CTR models.

Past approaches have tackled these challenges from different angles. Logistic regression and related generalized linear models gave interpretable baselines [10], but struggled with large, high-dimensional feature spaces. Factorization machines and deep learning methods incorporate feature interactions more effectively [4,9], but require substantial data and hyperparameter tuning to be robust

A. Bagherjeiran et al. (Eds.): AdKDD 2025, CCIS 2796, pp. 15–28, 2026.
https://doi.org/10.1007/978-3-032-16358-5_2

in sparse regimes. Gradient boosting frameworks such as XGBoost [1] can efficiently handle non-linearities and missing data, but they typically lack a built-in mechanism for temporal adaptation. Moreover, collaborative filtering (CF) has proven valuable in recommendation scenarios by leveraging user–item similarities, but the method falters when temporal trends or severe data sparsity are present [6].

In this paper, we propose an integrated solution that unifies Bayesian modeling, Dynamic Linear Models (DLMs), and collaborative filtering for CTR estimation. Our method uses a beta prior to capture uncertainty in sparse data within a DLM framework to model evolving CTR over time, then refines these posterior estimates using item-based collaborative filtering. We also introduce a hierarchical Bayesian component that shares information across related campaigns (e.g., those from the same advertiser), thereby mitigating cold-start problems and increasing accuracy. By systematically merging these elements, our approach reduces the adverse effects of data sparsity, adapts to temporal changes, and captures structural relationships between items and campaigns.

We evaluate our method on a large-scale dataset from a production RTB environment and benchmark it against well-established baselines: vanilla collaborative filtering, random forests, and XGBoost. Experimental results show that our framework achieves state-of-the-art performance in terms of log-loss and mean-squared error, outperforming alternatives by a considerable margin. Further analysis reveals that each component—such as the beta prior, the DLM smoothing, and the collaborative filtering step—contributes distinct benefits to the final model. Crucially, our pipeline remains computationally feasible for practical deployment, as both the DLM and CF steps are highly parallel and the Bayesian updates rely on conjugate priors, enabling efficient runtimes even under real-time requirements and the non-stationary nature of the online advertising ecosystem.

2 Related Work

CTR prediction lies at the core of many recommender systems and RTB platforms, driving advertising revenue and user satisfaction. A rich body of literature has explored methods ranging from classical regression techniques to sophisticated deep learning architectures, each addressing different aspects of sparsity, feature representation, or temporal adaptation. In this section, we review representative advances in CTR modeling, emphasizing both established baselines and recent progress toward integrated, adaptive models.

Generalized Linear and Tree-Based Methods. Early CTR optimization systems often relied on logistic regression (LR) for CTR estimation due to its interpretability and ability to incorporate large numbers of sparse features [10]. Meanwhile, tree-based ensemble methods gained traction by capturing non-linear feature interactions [5]. Approaches like Gradient Boosting Machines (GBMs) and XGBoost [1] streamlined training and inference, demonstrating strong performance on public benchmarks and real-world production logs. Although effective in handling complex feature patterns, these methods commonly treat each observation as temporally independent, relying on feature engineering or retraining for any time-varying behavior.

Factorization and Deep Learning Approaches. Factorization Machines (FMs) [9] extended linear models by explicitly modeling pairwise feature interactions with linear complexity. Deep learning then pushed this idea further, using embedding layers for sparse categorical features and neural networks for complex, high-order interactions. Models such as DeepFM [4], Wide&Deep [2], and DIN [13] found some success by automatically learning salient feature interactions and user interest representations from massive datasets. Nevertheless, these approaches assume stationarity or rely on periodically refreshed models, leaving them vulnerable to performance degradation when user preferences change.

Collaborative Filtering and Matrix Factorization. Borrowing from recommendation systems, CF posits that users with similar historical engagement patterns exhibit similar future behavior [7]. Matrix factorization techniques decompose the (user, item) ratings matrix into latent factors, effectively handling data sparsity [8]. Follow-up research introduced temporal extensions (TimeSVD++), capturing evolving user and item dynamics [6]. However, conventional CF methods often assume relatively stable preference structures, lack explicit uncertainty quantification and require significant modifications for application in RTB contexts.

Bayesian Modeling and Hierarchical Structures. Bayesian methods handle data sparsity by introducing priors that capture parameter uncertainty. In CTR prediction, hierarchical Bayesian frameworks can pool statistical strength across related entities such as advertisers or product categories [3]. Gamma priors for precision or beta priors for click-rate parameters have proven effective in preventing overfitting in sparse regimes. Despite these advantages, purely Bayesian or hierarchical methods can struggle with large-scale temporal data unless carefully optimized.

Temporal Adaptation via State-Space Models. Time-varying models incorporate sequential structure to adapt to user preference drift. Kalman filtering and Dynamic Linear Models (DLMs) [11] provide a probabilistic mechanism for updating beliefs about latent states over time. In online advertising, they can track CTR fluctuations driven by seasonal or campaign-related factors. However, DLMs alone do not fully exploit cross-campaign or cross-item signals, nor directly address unbalanced data when certain user-item pairs are underrepresented.

Reinforcement Learning and Bandit Perspectives. Recent work interprets ad allocation as a sequential decision-making problem, framing CTR prediction within multi-armed bandit or reinforcement learning (RL) paradigms [12].

These approaches dynamically update bidding strategies to maximize cumulative reward (e.g., clicks or conversions), often modeling the underlying user response stochastically. While RL-based methods can excel at balancing exploration and exploitation, they typically require a reliable reward model and careful sample-efficiency tuning, which is challenging in extremely sparse settings.

Our Contributions in Context. In contrast to purely static ML models, purely Bayesian frameworks, or purely RL-based strategies, our work bridges multiple elements to tackle real-world CTR estimation holistically:

- We adopt a *beta-based prior* to handle item-level or user-level data sparsity, ensuring robust uncertainty estimates.
- We embed *DLM updates* for smoothing temporal fluctuations, reducing the cost of frequent retraining.
- We refine these posterior estimates using *collaborative filtering*, exploiting cross-campaign or cross-item relationships.
- We incorporate a *hierarchical Bayesian model* to share information across related campaigns (e.g., from the same advertiser), mitigating cold-start and rare-event scenarios.

As a result, our approach not only captures evolving CTR dynamics but also addresses data scarcity and latent structure in large-scale RTB environments. Our experimental evaluation demonstrates superior performance against strong baselines, enabling practical use in real-world online advertising systems where speed, scalability, and adaptability are essential.

3 Methodology

This section describes our unified approach to CTR estimation, integrating beta-based Bayesian priors, a Kalman-filtered DLM, collaborative filtering (CF), and a hierarchical Bayesian framework. We begin with a high-level outline of how these components interact, then detail each step in the subsequent subsections. Algorithm 1 defines the setup and calls Algorithm 2 for the optimization loop.

3.1 Overview

We aim to estimate the click-through rate (CTR) for a given campaign, represented by user u, and an ad opportunity, represented by item i, at time t. Here, our units of analysis are campaigns and ad opportunities, but we adopt the conventional user-item notation prevalent in collaborative filtering literature. Our procedure operates offline in batches, and the final CTR matrix is retrieved in real-time bidding. Concretely:

Algorithm 1. Beta+DLM+CF Pipeline: Initialization and Deployment

Require: *Historical logs* $(c_{u,i,t}, n_{u,i,t})$ over time; *initial global priors* (α_0, β_0) from system logs; *hierarchical structure* (advertiser-level).
Ensure: *CTR estimates* $\widetilde{x}_{u,i,t}$ for real-time bidding.

(A) Calibrate Process Noise:
  Learn optimal Q that minimizes $\mathcal{L}_{\mathrm{KF}}$.
(B) Offline Iterative Updates Until Convergence (Algorithm 2):
  Run the repeated steps (Beta priors, DLM, CF, hierarchical updates, calibration) in Algorithm 2, monitoring changes in $(w_\alpha, w_\beta, \phi)$ and overall loss.
  Return Final CTR estimates $\widetilde{x}_{u,i,t}$ for each (u, i, t) at convergence.
(C) Offline-to-Online Deployment:
  (a) Once converged, store final CTR estimates $\widetilde{x}_{u,i,t}$ in a fast lookup table.
  (b) At bid time, retrieve $\widetilde{x}_{u,i,t}$ for the relevant (u, i) pair to score ad opportunities.

1. **Beta Hierarchical Model:** Each user–item pair has beta-based parameters, with hyperpriors across advertisers (or other groupings) to stabilize estimates in sparse scenarios.
2. **DLM (Kalman Filter) Fit:** A Gaussian DLM is run separately to produce a posterior CTR for each (u, i) at each time t, capturing temporal changes day by day.
3. **CF on the DLM Posterior:** We treat the DLM-updated CTR matrix as input to item-based CF. Neighbor similarities (scaled by impressions; i.e., the number of times the ad has been shown) refine each posterior estimate, partially blending in the collaborative signals.
4. **Global Mixture with Beta:** Finally, a single global mixing parameter combines the beta posterior mean for each pair (u, i) with the CF-refined DLM estimate. This ensures that beta priors remain influential for pairs with less data, while the DLM and CF steps drive estimates where observational evidence is stronger.

Although each step can be updated efficiently with local or gradient-based methods, the presence of collaborative filtering and global mixing means the overall model is not strictly conjugate. Attaining a fully conjugate solution would require handling global item–item dependencies in closed-form, which quickly becomes intractable for large-scale data. In practice, however, the partial conjugacy in beta–binomial updates and Gaussian DLM provides strong computational advantages, allowing us to handle real-world volumes without MCMC sampling or variational EM.

Algorithm 2. Beta+DLM+CF Iterative Steps (Repeated Until Convergence)

Beta Prior Initialization:

For each (u, i), set

$$\alpha_{u,i} = c_{u,i} + w_\alpha \, \alpha_0, \qquad \beta_{u,i} = \big(n_{u,i} - c_{u,i}\big) + w_\beta \, \beta_0.$$

Solve $\min \mathcal{L}_{\text{prior}}$ to update w_α, w_β.

Kalman Filter (DLM) Step:

(a) Predict:

$$\widehat{x}_{u,i,t|t-1} = \widehat{x}_{u,i,t-1}, \quad P_{u,i,t|t-1} = P_{u,i,t-1} + Q_{u,i}.$$

(b) Compute Kalman Gain:

$$K_{u,i,t} = \frac{P_{u,i,t|t-1}}{P_{u,i,t|t-1} + R_{u,i,t}}.$$

(c) Update:

$$\widehat{x}_{u,i,t} = \widehat{x}_{u,i,t|t-1} + K_{u,i,t}\big(z_{u,i,t} - \widehat{x}_{u,i,t|t-1}\big),$$

$$P_{u,i,t} = \big(1 - K_{u,i,t}\big) \, P_{u,i,t|t-1}.$$

Collaborative Filtering (Inverse Beta Variance):

For each (u, i), compute

$$w_{u,i} = \frac{\big(\alpha_{u,i} + \beta_{u,i}\big)^2 \big(\alpha_{u,i} + \beta_{u,i} + 1\big)}{\alpha_{u,i} \, \beta_{u,i}},$$

the reciprocal of the beta variance.

Calculate item–item similarities $\text{sim}(i, j)$ using $w_{u,i} \, w_{u,j}$ and $\widehat{x}_{u,i,t}$ from the DLM.

Update each CTR:

$$\widetilde{x}_{u,i,t} = \frac{\sum_j \text{sim}(i, j) \, \widehat{x}_{u,j,t}}{\sum_j \big|\text{sim}(i, j)\big|}.$$

Hierarchical Bayesian Updates:

Incorporate hierarchical priors on (w_α, w_β) and (α_0, β_0).

Update $x_{\text{final}}(u, i, t) = \phi \, p_{\text{beta}}(u, i) + (1 - \phi) \, \widetilde{x}_{u,i,t}$.

Solve $\min \Big[\mathcal{L}_{\text{prior}} + \mathcal{L}_{\text{CF}} + \mathcal{L}_{\text{KF}} + \lambda_p \big(w_\alpha^2 + w_\beta^2 + \phi^2\big)\Big]$.

Check Convergence:

If changes in $(w_\alpha, w_\beta, \phi)$ or the total loss are below threshold, end. Else, repeat.

3.2 Beta Priors: $(\alpha_{u,i}, \beta_{u,i})$ Alpha-Beta

To model the prior distribution on $\mathrm{CTR}_{u,i}$ (the click-through rate for user u on item i), we adopt a $\mathrm{Beta}(\alpha_{u,i}, \beta_{u,i})$ form. This beta prior incorporates both the observed clicks/impressions and a *global* system-level prior captured by (α_0, β_0). The values of α_0 and β_0 are derived from historical log data *at the start of the process*, providing a consistent global reference point for all user–item pairs. Concretely,

$$\alpha_{u,i} = c_{u,i} + w_\alpha \alpha_0, \qquad \beta_{u,i} = \left(n_{u,i} - c_{u,i}\right) + w_\beta \beta_0,$$

where $c_{u,i}$ is the number of clicks and $n_{u,i}$ is the number of impressions for campaign u on item i. The learnable weights (w_α, w_β) ensure that the global prior does not dominate the data, especially in sparse regimes, by minimizing the negative log-likelihood of the prior.

Negative Log-Likelihood of the Beta Prior. For a single pair (u, i), the negative log-likelihood is

$$\ell_{\mathrm{prior}}^{(u,i)} = -\, c_{u,i} \ln\left(\tfrac{\alpha_{u,i}}{\alpha_{u,i}+\beta_{u,i}}\right) - \left(n_{u,i} - c_{u,i}\right) \ln\left(\tfrac{\beta_{u,i}}{\alpha_{u,i}+\beta_{u,i}}\right).$$

Rewriting,

$$\ell_{\mathrm{prior}}^{(u,i)} = -\, c_{u,i}\left[\ln(\alpha_{u,i}) - \ln(\alpha_{u,i} + \beta_{u,i})\right] - (n_{u,i} - c_{u,i})\left[\ln(\beta_{u,i}) - \ln(\alpha_{u,i} + \beta_{u,i})\right].$$

The partial derivatives with respect to w_α and w_β involve the chain rule applied to $\alpha_{u,i}$ and $\beta_{u,i}$. Specifically, for the hierarchical weights w_α and w_β, we have:

$$\frac{\partial \mathcal{L}_{\mathrm{prior}}}{\partial w_\alpha} = \sum_{(u,i)} c_{u,i} \cdot \frac{1}{\alpha_{u,i}} \cdot \frac{\partial \alpha_{u,i}}{\partial w_\alpha} - n_{u,i} \cdot \frac{1}{\alpha_{u,i} + \beta_{u,i}} \cdot \frac{\partial(\alpha_{u,i} + \beta_{u,i})}{\partial w_\alpha},$$

and similarly for w_β.

Summing this cost over *all* (u, i) yields the overall prior loss,

$$\mathcal{L}_{\mathrm{prior}} = \sum_{(u,i)} \ell_{\mathrm{prior}}^{(u,i)}.$$

We update (w_α, w_β) via gradient-based methods until convergence, ensuring that the final priors respect the data while retaining the global baseline context from (α_0, β_0).

3.3 Kalman Filtering for Temporal Dynamics

To handle temporal variation in campaign–item CTRs, we adopt a Dynamic Linear Model (DLM). At time t, the observed CTR $z_{u,i,t}$ is treated as a noisy measurement of a latent state $x_{u,i,t}$, which evolves according to

$$x_{u,i,t} = x_{u,i,t-1} + \omega_{u,i,t}, \quad z_{u,i,t} = x_{u,i,t} + \nu_{u,i,t},$$

where $\omega_{u,i,t} \sim \mathcal{N}(0, Q_{u,i})$ is the process noise, and $\nu_{u,i,t} \sim \mathcal{N}(0, R_{u,i,t})$ is the measurement noise. The standard Kalman update recursions yield a posterior estimate $\widehat{x}_{u,i,t}$ of the latent CTR. In practice, the measurement variance $R_{u,i,t}$ approximates a binomial proportion:

$$R_{u,i,t} \approx \frac{\widehat{x}_{u,i,t|t-1}\left(1-\widehat{x}_{u,i,t|t-1}\right)}{n_{u,i,t}},$$

where $n_{u,i,t}$ is the number of impressions at time t.

Process Noise Calibration. Although one could define $Q_{u,i} = \exp(\theta_{u,i})$ and optimize a distinct parameter $\theta_{u,i}$ for each user–item pair, we instead selects a *single global* σ^2 for the sake of computational tractability. We perform a grid search for Q over a range of candidate values and choose the one minimizing a Kalman-filter SSE. Formally,

$$\min_{Q} \mathcal{L}_{\mathrm{KF}} = \sum_{t,i \in \mathrm{top}\text{-}k} \left[\frac{\left(z_{i,t}-\widehat{x}_{i,t|t-1}\right)^2}{P_{i,t|t-1}+R_{i,t}} + \ln\left(P_{i,t|t-1}+R_{i,t}\right)\right],$$

where $P_{i,t|t-1} = P_{i,t-1} + Q$ is the prior state uncertainty for item i, and $z_{i,t}$ is the observed CTR. After identifying the Q value that best fits these top-k items, we apply it globally to every campaign–item pair in the analytic pipeline. This strategy balances numerical tractability with robust smoothing, obviating the need for item-specific process noise estimates and preventing extreme Q values in sparse regions of the dataset.

3.4 Collaborative Filtering with Inverse-Variance Weights

Given $\widehat{x}_{u,i,t}$, the DLM posterior $x_{u,i,t}$ mean for each campaign u and item i at time t, we refine those estimates via *item-based* collaborative filtering (CF) on *centered* data. Each pair (u, i) receives a beta-based weight:

$$w_{u,i} = \frac{\left(\alpha_{u,i}+\beta_{u,i}\right)^2\left(\alpha_{u,i}+\beta_{u,i}+1\right)}{\alpha_{u,i}\,\beta_{u,i}},$$

which is the reciprocal of the variance of the beta distribution. Items with sparse or volatile data thus have smaller $w_{u,i}$ and exert less influence on other items.

Weighted Cosine Similarity on Centered Vectors. To compare items i and j, we first *center* each item's DLM posteriors across campaigns:

$$x'_{u,i,t} = \hat{x}_{u,i,t} - \bar{\hat{x}}_{i,t},$$

where $\bar{x}_{i,t}$ is item i's mean DLM posterior CTR across users at time t. Then, we incorporate the beta weights in a *weighted cosine similarity*:

$$\mathrm{sim}_w(i,j) = \frac{\sum_u w_{u,i}\, w_{u,j} \left(x'_{u,i,t}\right)\left(x'_{u,j,t}\right)}{\sqrt{\sum_u \left(w_{u,i}\, x'_{u,i,t}\right)^2}\sqrt{\sum_u \left(w_{u,j}\, x'_{u,j,t}\right)^2}}.$$

Hence, each item's column is effectively scaled by $w_{u,i}$ before taking the dot products. Once we obtain $\text{sim}_w(i, j)$ for all pairs, we update the CTR estimate for user u on item i via:

$$\widetilde{x}_{u,i,t} = \frac{\sum_j \text{sim}_w(i, j)\, x_{u,j,t}}{\sum_j \left|\text{sim}_w(i, j)\right|}.$$

The denominator normalizes by the sum of absolute similarities so that high-similarity neighbors have more impact. One may also impose a top-k truncation on neighbors to reduce computational overhead. This CF step thus blends time-aware DLM updates with beta-based inverse-variance weighting, providing robust, neighbor-driven refinements in sparse settings.

3.5 Hierarchical Bayesian Modeling

Campaigns from the same advertiser often share thematic designs or targeting constraints. To leverage these similarities, we incorporate hierarchical gamma priors on the beta weights (w_α, w_β) and on (α_0, β_0) for each advertiser by pooling data across multiple campaigns:

$$w_\alpha \sim \text{Gamma}(a_\alpha, b_\alpha), \qquad w_\beta \sim \text{Gamma}(a_\beta, b_\beta).$$

These hyperpriors reduce variance and mitigate cold-start problems for newly added campaigns. They may be fitted via gradient-based methods.

Blending Beta Posterior and DLM State. In addition to the hierarchical structure on (w_α, w_β) and (α_0, β_0), we define a mixture to combine the beta-based posterior mean with the DLM-updated CTR. Specifically, for each campaign–item pair (u, i), let

$$p_{\text{beta}}(u, i) = \frac{\alpha_{u,i}}{\alpha_{u,i} + \beta_{u,i}},$$

represent the beta posterior mean derived from $(\alpha_{u,i}, \beta_{u,i})$. Then, we introduce a global mixture parameter $\phi \in [0, 1]$. The final CTR prediction is:

$$x_{\text{final}}(u, i, t) = \phi \left[p_{\text{beta}}(u, i)\right] + (1 - \phi)\, \widetilde{x}_{u,i,t},$$

where $\widetilde{x}_{u,i,t}$ is the CF-based state. Hence, the hierarchical Bayesian framework supplies campaign-level priors for (w_α, w_β) and baseline hyperparameters (α_0, β_0), while the DLM smoothly adapts CTR estimates over time and the CF step incorporates item exploration. The mixture factor ϕ balances these two components, finding the optimal mixture between the total accrued information through the beta posterior and the time-varying DLM+CF process.

3.6 Offline Training and Real-Time Scoring

All steps run in a batch pipeline, collecting daily (or sub-daily) logs to update $(w_\alpha, w_\beta, \phi)$, Q, CF similarities, and hierarchical parameters. The final CTR estimates $x_{\text{final}}(u, i, t)$ are then cached for real-time retrieval, providing swift inferences for high-frequency bidding requests.

4 Experiments and Results

We conduct an extensive set of experiments on a large-scale *mobile display advertising* dataset sampled from InMarket's Demand-Side Platform (DSP). Our primary goal is to investigate whether combining beta-based priors, Dynamic Linear Models (DLMs), and collaborative filtering (CF) with inverse variance weighting can surpass established baselines in click-through rate (CTR) prediction accuracy. This section outlines the data properties, experimental protocols, evaluation criteria, and the final performance results on the test set.

4.1 Dataset and Experimental Protocol

Data Collection and Summary. We use impression-and-click logs from InMarket's DSP, covering campaigns (users) and ad opportunities (items) over **July 1, 2024** to **September 30, 2024**. Each record comprises:

- **Campaign ID** (u),
- **Item/App ID** (i),
- **Impressions** $(n_{u,i,t})$,
- **Clicks** $(c_{u,i,t})$,
- **Day-level timestamp** (t).

The dataset is highly sparse and includes 1,438 unique campaigns, 18,653 items, and 36 advertisers. In total, there are 588,457,330 impressions, 2,655,840 clicks, and an overall average CTR of 0.00451.

Time-Based Partitioning. We split the data chronologically into:

- **Training**: First 56 d (60%) of the log period,
- **Validation**: Next 18 d (20%),
- **Test**: Final 18 d (20%).

Hence, the training set covers early July to late August; the validation set spans the subsequent 18 d; and the test set covers the remainder of September. We optimize hyperparameters on the validation set, then assess final model performance on the test set.

Competing Methods. We evaluate the following models:

- **Beta+DLM+CF** (*ours*): Integrates beta-based priors, temporal smoothing via a Kalman-filtered DLM, and CF weighted by the inverse beta variance.
- **Beta+CF**: An ablated version of our approach that uses beta priors in CF but omits the DLM time-series component.
- **DLM+CF**: Another ablated version that applies a DLM for temporal updates plus CF, but without beta priors.
- **Vanilla CF**: A standard item-based collaborative filter without beta-based uncertainty or temporal modeling.
- **Random Forest**: A tree-ensemble classifier using campaign/item IDs as categorical features, ignoring explicit temporal adaptation.
- **XGBoost**: A boosted-tree classifier recognized for strong performance in many CTR tasks, similarly lacking an explicit temporal mechanism.

4.2 Evaluation Metrics

We report both MSE and log loss metrics. The log loss provides a stronger penalization for rare events than most other measures:

Log-Loss (Binary Cross-Entropy).

$$\text{LogLoss} = -\frac{\sum_{(u,i,t)}\Big[c_{u,i,t}\ln(\widetilde{x}_{u,i,t}) + \big(n_{u,i,t} - c_{u,i,t}\big)\ln\big(1 - \widetilde{x}_{u,i,t}\big)\Big]}{\sum_{(u,i,t)} n_{u,i,t}}.$$

Log-loss heavily penalizes poor probability estimates.

Mean Squared Error (MSE).

$$\text{MSE} = \sum_{(u,i,t)} \left(\widetilde{x}_{u,i,t} - \frac{c_{u,i,t}}{n_{u,i,t}}\right)^2 \Big/ \sum_{(u,i,t)} 1,$$

which provides a simple global measure of prediction accuracy.

4.3 Test Set Results

Table 1 summarizes each method's performance (log-loss and MSE) on the test set. Notably, we incorporate two partial variants of our final pipeline—*Beta+CF* and *DLM+CF*—to illustrate the incremental gains from combining beta priors and dynamic modeling.

Table 1. Test Set Performance: Log-Loss and MSE (lower is better). Our full **Beta+DLM+CF** approach achieves the best accuracy, demonstrating the combined value of beta priors and DLM smoothing.

Method	Log-Loss	MSE
Beta+DLM+CF	**0.025234**	**0.000144**
Beta+CF	0.029487	0.000185
DLM+CF	0.030523	0.000523
Vanilla CF	0.035877	0.000654
Random Forest	0.042545	0.000204
XGBoost	0.043481	0.000204

4.4 Discussion of Improvements

Impact of Beta Priors vs. DLM. Comparing **DLM+CF** (log-loss 0.030523) with **Beta+CF** (log-loss 0.029487) reveals that beta priors alone yield a larger improvement than DLM alone for these data. This highlights how uncertainty modeling via beta distributions can substantially mitigate sparse or cold-start conditions by preventing overconfident estimates.

Combination of Beta and DLM. Our full model, **Beta+DLM+CF**, outperforms both partial variants (*Beta+CF* and *DLM+CF*), underscoring the combined benefits of dynamic smoothing on top of beta-based priors. In particular, the log-loss drops from 0.029487 to 0.025234—a relative improvement of over 14%—once we include time-series adaptation in addition to beta's uncertainty mechanism.

Comparison to Tree Methods. Random forest and XGBoost yield higher log-loss (above 0.042) and slightly higher MSE, aligning with previous observations that purely feature-based classifiers often lack a built-in way to handle time-varying CTR or confidence weighting for sparse user-item pairs.

Vanilla CF vs. Weighted Approaches. Vanilla CF performs worse (0.035877 log-loss) than any version incorporating beta or DLM. This gap illustrates the importance of weighting edges by confidence (beta variance) and capturing time-series trends (DLM). The naive CF approach fails to handle heterogeneity across campaigns, leading to less reliable neighbor estimates.

4.5 Summary of Experimental Findings

The experimental results confirm that **Beta+DLM+CF** provides the most robust CTR predictions, with both beta priors and temporal smoothing offering clear advantages over partial or alternative methods. Each ablated variant (Beta+CF, DLM+CF) highlights a piece of our final pipeline's contribution. Overall, these findings motivate the integration of uncertainty modeling, dynamic adaptation, and collaborative filtering in next-generation programmatic advertising systems.

4.6 Runtime and Scalability

Another key advantage of our framework is its computational efficiency. Both the DLM updates and the item-based CF steps are embarrassingly parallel, allowing us to batch daily logs or distribute user–item pairs across multiple threads. Moreover, the Bayesian components (beta prior updates, hierarchical hyperparameters) use conjugate forms that yield closed-form updates.

On a 13th Gen Intel® Core™ i9-13900H laptop, the entire 90-day experiment (training + daily DLM + CF steps and convergence) finished in **1 h 47 min**. Once the model is fitted, generating CTR outputs for a single new day took only **0.077 s** per campaign, making this approach well-suited for daily or sub-daily updates in real-time bidding settings.

5 Conclusion

We have presented a new CTR prediction framework, *Beta+DLM+CF*, which unifies beta-based priors, a Dynamic Linear Model (DLM) for temporal smoothing, and collaborative filtering (CF) driven by inverse beta variance weighting. This combination addresses three key challenges in real-time bidding environments: uncertainty due to sparse user–item interactions, non-stationary user behavior over time, and the heterogeneous importance of different campaigns and items. By learning priors that adapt to data availability, accounting for temporal shifts with the Kalman filter, and emphasizing reliable (low-variance) neighbors in CF, the proposed system significantly improves log-loss and MSE relative to standard baselines.

Empirically, we demonstrated that our approach achieves state-of-the-art performance on a large-scale dataset, outperforming methods such as vanilla CF, item-average baselines, and strong tree-based classifiers (Random Forest, XGBoost). An ablation analysis further confirmed that removing any of our framework's components (e.g., beta priors, DLM smoothing, or variance-based CF) causes measurable deterioration in prediction accuracy. Moreover, the hierarchical Bayesian extension empowers the system to mitigate cold-start conditions by pooling statistical strength across related campaigns.

From a practical standpoint, the offline training plus real-time inference design ensures compatibility with high-frequency programmatic auctions, where computational speed is paramount. Our calibration procedures for process noise (Q) and hyperpriors (α_0, β_0) balance robustness with responsiveness to changes in user behavior.

Several promising directions remain for future exploration. First, we intend to integrate more advanced embeddings and contextual signals (e.g., user demographics or device types) into the CF step. Second, adapting reinforcement learning or bandit methods on top of Beta+DLM+CF could further optimize bidding policies, leveraging strong CTR predictions as a baseline while exploring novel ad placements. Lastly, scaling hierarchical priors to thousands of advertisers raises compelling research questions on distributed inference and approximate Bayesian techniques. We anticipate that continued refinement of these ideas will advance the field of CTR prediction, offering increasingly accurate and adaptive solutions for real-time advertising systems.

References

1. Chen, T., Guestrin, C.: XGBoost: a scalable tree boosting system. In: Proceedings of the 22nd ACM SIGKDD International Conference on Knowledge Discovery and Data Mining (KDD). pp. 785–794. ACM (2016). https://doi.org/10.1145/2939672.2939785
2. Cheng, H.T., et al.: Wide & deep learning for recommender systems. In: Proceedings of the 1st Workshop on Deep Learning for Recommender Systems, DLRS 2016, pp. 7–10. Association for Computing Machinery, New York (2016). https://doi.org/10.1145/2988450.2988454
3. Gelman, A., Carlin, J.B., Stern, H.S., Dunson, D.B., Vehtari, A., Rubin, D.B.: Bayesian Data Analysis. Chapman and Hall/CRC, second edition edn. (2006)
4. Guo, H., Tang, R., Ye, Y., Li, Z., He, X.: Deepfm: a factorization-machine based neural network for ctr prediction. In: Proceedings of the 26th International Joint Conference on Artificial Intelligence, pp. 1725–1731 (2017)
5. He, X., et al.: Practical lessons from predicting clicks on ads at facebook. In: International Workshop on Data Mining for Online Advertising (2014). https://api.semanticscholar.org/CorpusID:2999385
6. Koren, Y.: Collaborative filtering with temporal dynamics. In: Communications of the ACM, vol. 53, pp. 89–97 (2010)
7. Koren, Y., Bell, R., Volinsky, C.: Matrix factorization techniques for recommender systems. Computer **42**(8), 30–37 (2009). https://doi.org/10.1109/MC.2009.263
8. Patrick M. LeBlanc, David Banks, L.F.M.L.Z.T., Wu, Q.: Recommender systems: A review. J. Am. Statist. Associat. **119**(545), 773–785 (2024). https://doi.org/10.1080/01621459.2023.2279695
9. Rendle, S.: Factorization machines. In: 2010 IEEE International Conference on Data Mining, pp. 995–1000 (2010). https://api.semanticscholar.org/CorpusID:17265929
10. Richardson, M., Dominowska, E., Ragno, R.J.: Predicting clicks: estimating the click-through rate for new ads. In: The Web Conference (2007). https://api.semanticscholar.org/CorpusID:14669618
11. West, M., Harrison, J.: Bayesian forecasting and dynamic models. Springer (1997)
12. Zhao, Y., et al.: Multi-scenario combination based on multi-agent reinforcement learning to optimize the advertising recommendation system. In: 2024 5th International Conference on Artificial Intelligence and Electromechanical Automation IEEE (2024). https://doi.org/10.48550/2407.02759, https://arxiv.org/abs/2407.02759
13. Zhou, G., et al.: Deep interest evolution network for click-through rate prediction. Proceedings of the AAAI Conference on Artificial Intelligence, vol. 33, 5941–5948 (07 2019). https://doi.org/10.1609/aaai.v33i01.33015941

MTMD: A Multi-task Multi-domain Framework for Unified Ad Lightweight Ranking at Pinterest

Xiao Yang(✉), Peifeng Yin, Abe Engle, Jinfeng Zhuang, and Ling Leng

Pinterest Inc., 651 Brannan Street, San Francisco, CA, USA
{xyang,pyin,aengle,jzhuang,lleng}@pinterest.com

Abstract. The lightweight ad ranking layer, living after the retrieval stage and before the fine ranker, plays a critical role in the success of a cascaded ad recommendation system. Due to the fact that there are multiple optimization tasks depending on the ad domain, e.g., Click Through Rate (CTR) for click ads and Conversion Rate (CVR) for conversion ads, as well as multiple surfaces where an ad is served (home feed, search, or related item recommendation) with diverse ad products (shopping or standard ad); it is an essentially challenging problem in industry on how to do joint holistic optimization in the lightweight ranker, such that the overall platform's value, advertiser's value, and user's value are maximized.

Deep Neural Network (DNN)-based multitask learning (MTL) can handle multiple goals naturally, with each prediction head mapping to a particular optimization goal. However, in practice, it is unclear how to unify data from different surfaces and ad products into a single model. It is critical to learn domain-specialized knowledge and explicitly transfer knowledge between domains to make MTL effective. We present a **M**ulti-**T**ask **M**ulti-**D**omain (MTMD) architecture under the classic Two-Tower paradigm, with the following key contributions: 1) handle different prediction tasks, ad products, and ad serving surfaces in a unified framework; 2) propose a novel mixture-of-expert architecture to learn both specialized knowledge each domain and common knowledge shared between domains; 3) propose a domain adaption module to encourage knowledge transfer between experts; 4) constrain the modeling of different prediction tasks. MTMD improves the offline loss value by 12% to 36%, mapping to 2% online reduction in cost per click. We have deployed this single MTMD framework into production for Pinterest ad recommendation replacing 9 production models.

Keywords: Lightweight Ads Ranking · Multi-task Learning · Mixture-of-experts · Domain Adaptation · Deep Neural Networks

A. Bagherjeiran et al. (Eds.): AdKDD 2025, CCIS 2796, pp. 29–41, 2026.
https://doi.org/10.1007/978-3-032-16358-5_3

1 Introduction

The goal of modern online ad recommendation is to serve ad content that is highly personalized to user's interests, tastes, goals, and intent at the right time through the right funnel, such that user's value, advertiser's value, and platform's value are jointly maximized.

Modern advertising recommendation is often a cascading system [5], divided into retrieval, lightweight ranking[1], heavyweight ranking, and auction stages. The latency requirement of each layer is different depending on the number of ads entering and surviving that stage. Figure 2 presents the scale in a typical delivery funnel. The lightweight ranking tier usually has millions to billions of ads as input. Due to the latency requirement, the lightweight ranker often uses a two-tower architecture [2,6], which allows the dot product between the query embedding and the item embedding as a fast inference function. Its performance is on the critical path to high-quality ad recommendation (Fig. 1).

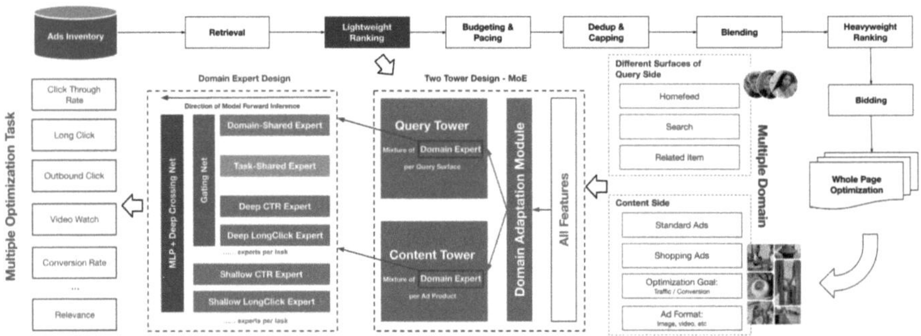

Fig. 1. Illustration of online ad serving system, where the lightweight ranking is a middle tier optimizing all downstream goals. MTMD is a two-tower architecture that unifies both the input side (multiple domains) and the output side (multiple optimization tasks) based on a Mixture-of-Expert architecture.

However, it is a very challenging problem to improve lightweight ranking in practice. The first challenge is the alignment of the delivery funnel: even if lightweight ranking is measured better in some scientific metrics, the gain often diminishes if the latter heavyweight ranking is not respecting the changes. Lightweight and heavyweight models are often not trained together. Second, there are many ad domains in a real-world system, e.g., the query side has different surfaces (home feed or search) and users, while the content side has different ad products, formats, and optimization goals. The lightweight ranker

[1] Also referred by "pre-ranking", "early ranking", "coarse ranking", "retrieval ranking" etc. We choose the name "lightweight" in this paper to emphasize the fact that latency plays an important role in our design choices.

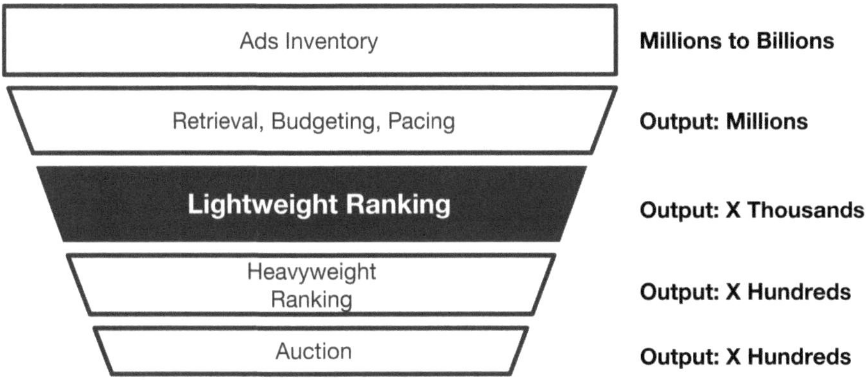

Fig. 2. The throughput of each stage in a typical ad delivery funnel. Two-tower based model has the advantage of fast inference when the throughput is high.

needs to handle them together as a single tier, with a model complexity budget to meet the latency requirement.

For the first alignment challenge, consistency-oriented lightweight ranking approaches have recently been proposed, to make ranking results similar to heavyweight ranking [12,16,18,24]. Our MTMD learning uses the prediction score from the heavyweight ranker as the label, which encourages funnel alignment in nature. We limit the scope of this paper to the second multi-domain challenge.

One common practice is to train a model per ad domain. This approach suffers from two problems: 1) data fragmentation: a single training example was used in separate models, either for different tasks (e.g., CTR and CVR) or for different surfaces (e.g., home feed and search). Each domain could have more training data if we can share all training data; 2) maintenance and development velocity: we have to try all domains if we hope to test a new innovation or migrate some models. Furthermore, there are often mix shift phenomena between different models, where one task or one surface is improved while another is harmed.

Multitask learning (MTL) [11,15,18,23] has been widely adopted to handle various optimization tasks jointly in industrial recommendation systems. However, naive handling of domain-specific features is suboptimal: When a feature is only available for a specific domain, the values of it are often set to certain default ones. Intuitively, having a more sophisticated domain adaptation module to handle missing values could improve model performance. When the input domains are very different from each other, both domain-specialized knowledge and common knowledge are required to maximize the power of MTL.

Specific to the model architecture, a general direction to improve two-tower models is to allow interaction modules between the query side and the item side [4,10,14,19,21,22]. For our scale, we can only afford the dot product as the inference function due to latency consideration, and we need embedding output as a potential feature feeding to the heavyweight ranker. We do not explore these interaction modules for the focus of this paper.

Putting together, we propose MTMD, a **M**ulti-**T**ask **M**ulti-**D**omain network for unified web-scale lightweight ad ranker following the two-tower framework. The core building block of our network is a **Domain Expert**, which itself is a mixture of experts (MoE) to handle the challenges in a vanilla data-mixing MTL approach. The major value in the proposed method includes the following:

- It has a series of fine-grained deep and shallow expert pairs for each prediction task, which explores the specialized knowledge of each task;
- It has domain-shared expert aiming to learn the common knowledge of different surfaces and ad products and allows more sophisticated domain adaptation to handle missing feature values;
- It has task-shared expert aiming to learn the common structure of different downstream prediction tasks;
- It has an expert routing layer to encourage different importance of experts.

With this Domain Expert as the foundational building block, the Query Tower in MTMD consists of N Domain Experts mapping to each ad serving surface (e.g., home feed, search, etc.), and the Item Tower consists of M Domain Experts mapping to each ad product type (e.g., shopping ad, traffic ad, etc.), followed by feedforward layers projecting tower output to the embedding vector for each task. In addition, we introduce the constraint of different prediction tasks; for instance, a Good Click event (GCTR, click duration is longer than 30 s) depends on a Click event (CTR).

We are able to deploy a single model in production replacing 9 lightweight ranking models on all surfaces, with significant gains in online metrics, including CTR (+**2.41**%), GCTR (+**3.06**%), CPC (−**1.96**%), and click volume (+**2.31**%), without increasing the impression of ads.

2 Design of MTMD

In this section, we present the network details of MTMD and the constrained modeling in MTL training.

2.1 Domain Expert

The design of Domain Expert focuses on the goal of unifying diverse input domains and output tasks, yet the resultant architecture should be composable and reusable for both the query side and the item side.

Formulation of Ad Domain. The definition of "domain" is platform dependent. Specific to Pinterest ad recommendation, an ad domain means the diverse input training data and the output prediction tasks of the lightweight ranking tier. Specifically, it is keyed by three dimensions:

- the **Surface** that an ad is served, including *home feed*, *search*, and *related item* recommendation;
- the **Ad Product** itself, including *standard ad*, which aims for personalized events like impression, click, etc., and *shopping ad*, which aims for offline conversion rate, i.e., a user purchases the item in this shopping ads;
- the **Prediction Task** of lightweight ranking, which includes *click* (CTR), *good/long click* (GCTR), *outbound click* (OBC), *conversion* (CVR), relevance, etc.;

The total number of ad domain will be $|\text{Surface}| * |\text{Ad Product}|$, where $|\cdot|$ is the number of values of a concrete variable. This definition is general enough to be applied in other social media or e-commerce platforms. MTMD aims to effectively handle this modeling diversity and complexity in a unified way so that all downstream heavyweight rankers can benefit from it. It should also significantly simplify the maintenance cost, compared to one model per domain.

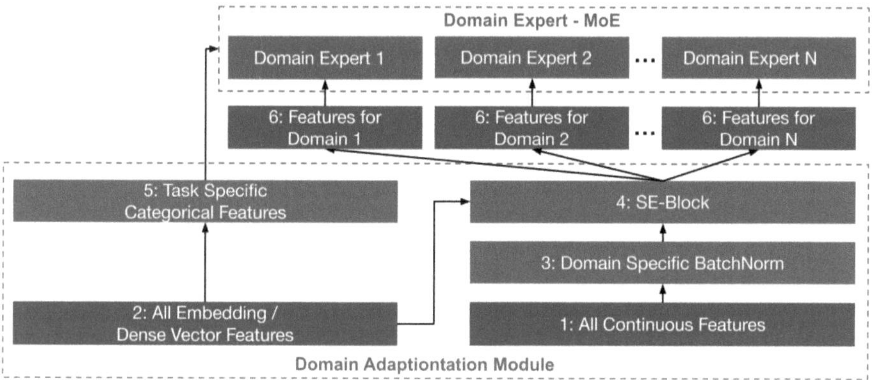

Fig. 3. The design of the ad Domain Adaptation module in MTMD based on the Squeeze-and-Excitation block.

Domain Adaptation. The first challenge we face is how to process the features from different domains effectively. Our recipe is presented in the blocks of Fig. 3. We use SE-Block from [8] so that different tasks/domains can capture the difference in the importance of features in different domains. For all the continuous features, e.g. the click count of an ad in a past rolling window, we add one BATCH-NORM [7] layer per domain before passing to the SE-Block.

Task-Specific Experts. Each task has a pair of deep and shallow experts:

Deep Expert consisting of a four-layer feedforward network (FFN) with dimensions $\{512, 256, 128, 128\}$. Each FFN layer consists of three sequential sublayers: fully connected linear projection [13], LAYER-NORM [1], and LEAKY-RELU activation [20] with negative slope 0.2. The goal of this expert is to learn a deep domain-specific knowledge.

Shallow Expert consisting of a two-layer FFN of size $\{128, 64\}$. While the deep expert works on all input features after domain adaption, this shallow expert only takes some high-level categorical features that describe the key ad product properties, for example, the ad product type (traffic ads or conversion ads), etc.

The total number of task-specific experts is $2 * |\text{Prediction Task}|$.

Domain-Shared and Task-Shared Expert. We have both domain-shared expert and task-shared expert, each consists of a four-layer FFN of size $\{512, 256, 128, 128\}$, whose output will pass through an expert routing layer to help learning global common knowledge of different domains. This shared expert treatment also encourages task-specific experts to learn specialized knowledge within each domain.

The Final Composition With the three types of expert, that is, task-specific deep expert, task-shared expert and domain-shared expert, we use a routing layer to learn the importance of experts, followed by a DCN module to explore the power of feature crossing. Specifically, the final composition includes:

Expert Routing layer consisting of a three-layer FFN of size $\{128, 64, |\text{Expert}|\}$ followed by a SOFTMAX function. The purpose of this layer is to capture the importance of the output of each expert, assuming that different experts should contribute differently with their specialized knowledge. This expert routing idea has recently shown great success in large models [3];

Deep Crossing Network (DCN) for feature crossing. It first applies LAYER-NORM to composited expert outputs, then applies the low-rank DCN module [17] on top of it to fully capture the crossing power of the feature crossing.

Final Embedding Generation: A linear layer that projects the output of DCN to the embedding emb_{deep} per prediction task. Simultaneously, the output from the task-specific shallow expert, $emb_{shallow}$, is directly concatenated with emb_{deep}. Note that the dot product of the final embedding can be interpreted as the sum of the dot product of emb_{deep} and the dot product of $emb_{shallow}$. This design allows the shallow expert to function as a calibration model, adjusting the logits from the deep networks. Finally, the output of Domain Expert is a dictionary where key is a prediction task and value is an embedding vector in Euclidian space.

Figure 4 presents the hierarchy of expert composition with three tasks CTR, GCTR, and OCTR as examples. It can be generalized to other tasks including CVR and relevance, etc.

2.2 Query Tower and Item Tower

With the Domain Expert design above, we are equipped to build our Query Tower and Item Tower following a two-tower architecture.

Our key recipe is to decouple their types of domain experts from each other and design the tower architecture based on the uniqueness of Pinterest data. However, the idea is generalizable to other ad platforms, too:

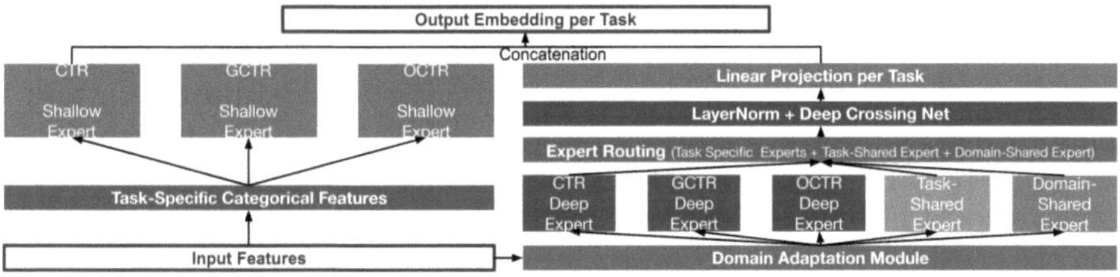

Fig. 4. Design of Domain Expert. **On the Left:** shallow expert per task. **On the Right:** After passing Domain Adaptation processing of features, it goes through task specific Deep Expert, Task-Shared Expert, and Domain-Shared Expert.

- On the query side, we aggregate the Domain Expert **by different ad serving surfaces**: Home feed, Search, and Related Pins (related item recommendation in general);
- On the item side, we aggregate the Domain Expert **by two different types of ad product**: Standard and Shopping ads.

Each domain expert has its own collection of input features decided by the type of this domain expert. For example, a shopping ad expert on the item side will only receive the shopping features after the domain adaptation module. During serving time, only a single domain expert is activated for each request, which leads to improved infrastructure efficiency. Figure 5 summarized the two-tower architecture.

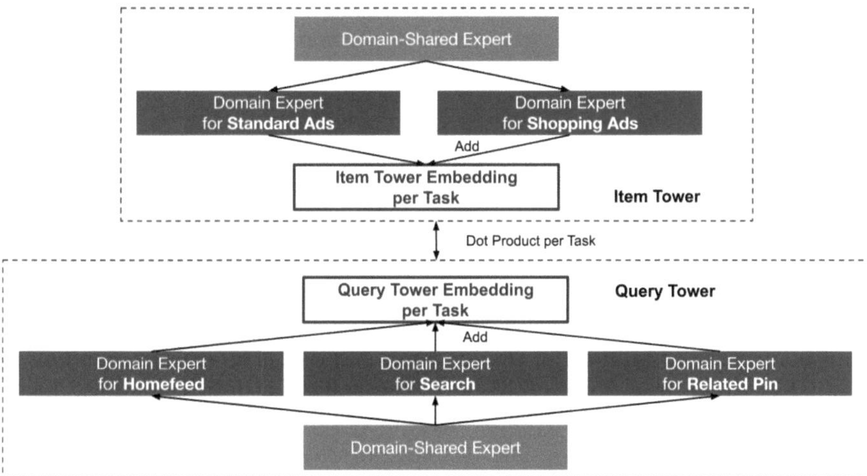

Fig. 5. The two tower arch based on Domain Expert.

2.3 Constrained Modeling

In a standard MTL (Multi-Task Learning) framework, each prediction task is equipped with its own Feed-Forward Network (FFN) layer to create embeddings specific to that task. These embeddings are then utilized in the dot product during inference, which essentially presumes that the tasks operate independently from one another. However, in our scenario, such a configuration ignores the conditional relationship between different prediction tasks. Taking the three types of clicks in Fig. 4 as an example, a long click (GCTR) should be conditioned on a click (CTR). The same is true for outbound clicks (OCTR). Moreover, an equal size of the output embedding dimension, which is 64 each task as in Sect. 2.1, does not reflect the importance of the more fundamental role of CTR.

We propose a Constrained Modeling between different tasks to solve the above two limitations. First, we introduce the dependency between tasks in the formulation:

$$\begin{aligned} P(\mathrm{CTR}) &= P(\mathrm{Click}|\mathrm{Impression}), \\ P(\mathrm{GCTR}) &= P\big(\mathrm{GCTR}|\mathrm{Impression}\big) \Rightarrow P\big(\mathrm{GCTR}|\mathrm{CTR}\big) * P(\mathrm{CTR}), \\ P(\mathrm{OCTR}) &= P\big(\mathrm{OCTR}|\mathrm{Impression}\big) \Rightarrow P\big(\mathrm{OCTR}|\mathrm{CTR}\big) * P(\mathrm{CTR}), \end{aligned}$$

In implementation, we use the KL-Divergence [9] between lightweight prediction score and the heavyweight prediction score as a loss function. By formulating GCTR and OCTR conditionally on CTR, the model can develop better understanding of CTR. GCTR and OCTR can also get causal benefits. Moreover, we used 128 dimensions for the CTR embedding, 32 for both the GCTR and the OCTR embedding, instead of an even 64 dimension for each task. We also use a larger weight on the loss of CTR prediction to further increase its importance in training.

3 Experiments and Results

3.1 Dataset and Experiment Setup

Our offline experiments are conducted on a subset of a large-scale production dataset. This evaluation data set has approximately hundreds of millions of samples and tens of millions of unique users per day. The training periods for our models range from 20 to 60 d, ensuring sufficient data for robust model training and evaluation. The online experiments are based on the online A/B experiment to evaluate the top-line business metrics.

The ground truth label in training is the heavyweight ranker prediction score instead of the user action labels. MTMD can be applied to both engagement models and conversion models. It has been launched for both traffic and conversion ads at Pinterest. We focus on the three engagement tasks in this section.

3.2 Offline Evaluation

We evaluated on three surfaces: home feed (HF), search (SR), and related Pin (RP), 2 ad product type: standard ads and shopping ads, and 3 engagement tasks: CTR, GCTR, and OCTR. The baseline are production two-tower models trained using data only on a single slice. Each tower in baseline is a multilayer feedforward network after feature pre-processing.

We explored KL-Divergence, LogMAE, MAE, BCE, etc. as offline evaluation metrics. Empirically, we have found that logMAE is stable and maps well to the online metric movement directionally. When it is positive in offline evaluation tables, it means it reduces LogMAE more.

Table 1. Offline improvement of LogMAE of MTMD on different ad domains for three engagement tasks. A positive number means it reduces LogMAE further.

Surface	Ad Type	CTR	GCTR	OCTR
home feed	shopping	35.65%	32.30%	N/A
home feed	standard	20.25%	36.66%	23.40%
related Pin	shopping	32.31%	31.06%	N/A
related Pin	standard	23.38%	22.65%	36.58%
search	shopping	16.84%	23.48%	N/A
search	standard	12.42%	23.69%	35.62%

Table 1 presents the change in the offline metric. We can observe that MTMD significantly improved performance in all tasks and all domains by a large margin between 12% and 36%. The MTMD model possesses a comparable number of embedding parameters and a reduced number of non-embedding parameters relative to all baseline models combined. This robust offline performance provides compelling evidence that a singular, unified model can surpass individual models by integrating fragmented data and employing a meticulously designed model architecture.

These offline results are very encouraging. To further assess the model performance in real-world large-scale scenario, we conduct an online A/B experiment to understand the impact on online business metrics such as CTR and CPC (Tables 2 and 5).

3.3 Online A/B Test

We evaluate the following business metrics in an online A/B setup, where users are randomly split into control and treatment groups. The control group is a production model and the treatment group is MTMD.

- CPC: cost per click on ad. Measures how much an advertiser pays for each click on their ad. The lower the better;

Table 2. Home feed VS Related Pin VS Search - Online A/B test results by ad serving surface.

	CPC	CTR	GCTR	OCTR	HDR	RPR
Home feed	**−2.95%**	**3.62%**	3.29%	4.77%	-0.21%	7.73%
Related Pin	**−1.60%**	**2.07%**	3.07%	2.32%	-0.13%	3.27%
Search	**−1.60%**	**2.07%**	3.07%	2.32%	-0.13%	3.27%

Table 3. Standard ads VS Shopping ads - Online A/B test results by ad product type.

	CPC	CTR	GCTR	OCTR	HDR	RPR
Standard	**−1.79%**	**2.17%**	2.84%	2.72%	-0.01%	4.46%
Shopping	**−2.12%**	**2.99%**	3.73%	2.93%	-2.45%	5.19%

- CTR: ad clickthrough rate. It is important business metric for user experience;
- GCTR: the rate an ad is clicked and a user stays ¿30 s on it;
- OCTR: CTR for the ad that goes to a 3rd party site;
- HDR: hide rate of this ad. The lower the better;
- RPR: ad repin rate. It is a Pinterest-specific feature that strongly correlates with user experience;

Note that we do not track revenue, presumably the most important ad metric, because we force identical budget over control and treatment groups to eliminate the impact of budget cannibalization. We highlight the metric changes in CPC and CTR in bold font because they are the most crucial, indicating the business value and user value, respectively.

Significant Platform-Level Lift. Overall MTMD reduces CPC and significantly increases CTR, which is one of the most significant launches in years for the lightweight ranking tier. The three prediction tasks CTR, GCTR, and OCTR are all improved at the same time, while the repin rate is significantly improved by $3+\%$ and the hide rate is slightly decreased. The online gain is also consistent across

- Serving Surface: all three surfaces saw a significant CPC reduction with an increase in CTR;
- Product Type: table 3 showed that CPC and CTR are improved significantly on both standard and shopping ad;

Table 4. Click ads VS Conversion ads - Online A/B test results by ad optimization goal.

	CPC	CTR	GCTR	OCTR	HDR	RPR
Click	**−1.97%**	**3.49%**	4.67%	4.30%	0.12%	7.78%
Conversion	**−1.88%**	**1.87%**	2.18%	1.79%	-0.71%	3.07%

Table 5. Constrained Modeling - Online A/B test results in percentage with MTMD model architecture as baseline.

	CPC	CTR	GCTR	OCTR	HDR	RPR
Home feed	**−0.81%**	**0.61%**	0.79%	0.62%	-2.81%	0.65%
Related Pin	0.02%	**0.43%**	−0.18%	0.45%	−6.15%	0.22%
Search	0.37%	−0.18%	−0.65%	−0.17%	4.37%	−1.03%
Standard	−0.08%	0.15%	−0.23%	0.13%	-3.86%	−1.13%
Shopping	**−0.37%**	**0.60%**	0.56%	0.63%	−1.86%	0.87%

- Optimization Goal: MTMD increases the CTR of the click ad by $+\mathbf{3.49}\%$, and reduces the CPC of the conversion ads by $-\mathbf{1.88}\%$.

Performance by Constrained Modeling. The offline gain of constrained modeling is marginal after the 5th bucket. We conduct a separate online A/B experiment with MTMD as the baseline, to determine whether constrained modeling can further enhance the value of MTMD. Table 5 shows that constrained modeling can bring statistically significant gains in CPC and CTR.

3.4 Ablation Study

We present ablation studies measured by LogMAE to justify design choices. One factor is removed at a time to assess how the offline metric would change. The results are summarized in Table 6. We did not conduct online A/B experiments for this purpose because of the large number of variants.

Table 6. Offline improvement of LogMAE of different factors on the top ranked buckets.

	0	1	2	3	4	all
DomainAdapt	3.71%	3.53%	3.67%	3.88%	4.38%	**3.86%**
DCN V2	0.90%	0.99%	1.15%	1.34%	1.71%	**1.24%**
Normalization	2.36%	2.50%	2.64%	2.64%	2.84%	**2.61%**
DownSampling	-0.23%	-0.29%	-0.84%	0.15%	-0.12%	-0.26%

The order of impact is Domain Adaptation ¿ Proper Normalization ¿ DCN Feature Crossing. The smaller embedding dimension and the downsampling of the data can slightly hurt the performance. Specifically,

- Domain adaptation: brings $+\mathbf{3.86}\%$ improvement to LogMAE. This confirms the motivation that the transfer of feature representations between domains helps MTL;

- DCN crossing: the DCN V2 crossing module applied to the output of deep experts further improves the loss by **+1.24%**;
- Proper Normalization: contributes to **+2.61%** loss improvement, Pre-norm is better than post-norm;
- Larger embedding dimension is better: We evaluated different dimensions of the embeddings of the two-tower output. It shows a clear trend for performance-wise $64 > 48 > 32$.

4 Conclusion and Future Works

In this paper, we present a unified Multi-Task Multi-Domain (MTMD) lightweight ranking framework. The core design component is a Domain Expert, which adapts feature processing with respect to various domains, ensembles four different types of expert, and crosses the expert outputs using DCN V2. With this Domain Expert, we composite the pin tower by the type of ad product and the query tower by the surface an ad is served. This MTMD model replaced nine models in production and delivered a significant reduction in CPC and a substantial increase in CTR during the online A / B experiment. MTMD has been the lightweight ranking model in production at Pinterest.

In the future, we will improve our design in the two orthogonal directions: The first is the **alignment of the delivery funnel**, where the goal is to make the output of lightweight ranking and heavyweight ranking more consistent for better ad delivery efficiency. The other direction is to **allow better interaction** between the query tower and the pin tower to make the model more effective in capturing the personalized needs of the users.

Acknowledgments. We thank Hari Venkatesan for his support in the development of MTMD.

References

1. Ba, J.L., Kiros, J.R., Hinton, G.E.: Layer normalization (2016). https://arxiv.org/abs/1607.06450
2. Bromley, J., et al.: Signature verification using A “siamese” time delay neural network. Int. J. Pattern Recognit Artif Intell. **7**(4), 669–688 (1993)
3. Dai, D., et al.: Deepseekmoe: towards ultimate expert specialization in mixture-of-experts language models. In: ACL, pp. 1280–1297 (2024)
4. Dong, Z., et al.: Exploring dual encoder architectures for question answering. In: Goldberg, Y., Kozareva, Z., Zhang, Y. (eds.) EMNLP, pp. 9414–9419 (2022)
5. Gallagher, L., Chen, R., Blanco, R., Culpepper, J.S.: Joint optimization of cascade ranking models. In: WSDM, pp. 15–23 (2019)
6. Huang, P., He, X., Gao, J., Deng, L., Acero, A., Heck, L.P.: Learning deep structured semantic models for web search using clickthrough data. In: CIKM, pp. 2333–2338 (2013)

7. Ioffe, S., Szegedy, C.: Batch normalization: accelerating deep network training by reducing internal covariate shift. In: ICML. JMLR Workshop and Conference Proceedings, vol. 37, pp. 448–456. JMLR.org (2015)
8. Jiang, Y., et al.: Adaptive domain interest network for multi-domain recommendation. In: CIKM, pp. 3212–3221 (2022)
9. Kullback, S., Leibler, R.A.: On Information and Sufficiency. Ann. Math. Stat. **22**(1), 79–86 (1951)
10. Li, X., et al.: Inttower: the next generation of two-tower model for pre-ranking system. In: CIKM, pp. 3292–3301 (2022)
11. Ma, J., Zhao, Z., Yi, X., Chen, J., Hong, L., Chi, E.H.: Modeling task relationships in multi-task learning with multi-gate mixture-of-experts. In: KDD, pp. 1930–1939 (2018)
12. Qin, J., et al.: Rankflow: joint optimization of multi-stage cascade ranking systems as flows. In: SIGIR, pp. 814–824 (2022)
13. Rosenblatt, F.: The perceptron: a probabilistic model for information storage and organization in the brain. Psychol. Rev. **65**(6), 386–408 (1958). https://doi.org/10.1037/h0042519
14. Su, L., et al.: Beyond two-tower matching: learning sparse retrievable cross-interactions for recommendation. In: SigIR, pp. 548–557 (2023)
15. Tang, H., Liu, J., Zhao, M., Gong, X.: Progressive layered extraction (PLE): a novel multi-task learning (MTL) model for personalized recommendations. In: RecSys, pp. 269–278 (2020)
16. Tang, J., Wang, K.: Ranking distillation: learning compact ranking models with high performance for recommender system. In: KDD, pp. 2289–2298 (2018)
17. Wang, R., et al.: DCN V2: improved deep & cross network and practical lessons for web-scale learning to rank systems. In: WWW, pp. 1785–1797 (2021)
18. Wang, X., et al.: Towards the better ranking consistency: a multi-task learning framework for early stage ads ranking. In: AdKDD, vol. 3556 (2023)
19. Wang, Z., Zhao, L., Jiang, B., Zhou, G., Zhu, X., Gai, K.: COLD: towards the next generation of pre-ranking system. CoRR abs/ arXiv: 2007.16122 (2020). https://arxiv.org/abs/2007.16122
20. Xu, B., Wang, N., Chen, T., Li, M.: Empirical evaluation of rectified activations in convolutional network (2015). https://arxiv.org/abs/1505.00853
21. Yantao Yu, Weipeng Wang, Z.F.D.X.: A dual augmented two-tower model for online large-scale recommendation. In: DLP-KDD (2021)
22. Zhai, J., et al.: Revisiting neural retrieval on accelerators. In: KDD, pp. 5520–5531 (2023)
23. Zhao, Z., et al.: Recommending what video to watch next: a multitask ranking system. In: RecSys, pp. 43–51 (2019)
24. Zhao, Z., et al.: COPR: consistency-oriented pre-ranking for online advertising. In: CIKM, pp. 4974–4980 (2023)

Mitigating Position Bias in Click Predictor Models: A Novel Downsampling Approach for Enhanced Accuracy and Efficiency

Phuong Ha Nguyen[1(✉)], Djordje Gligorijevic[2], Hung Nguyen[3], Sheng Shen[3], Zhenke Xi[3], and Abraham Bagherjeiran[3]

[1] eBay Inc, SJ, USA
phuongha.ntu@gmail.com
[2] Meta Inc, SJ, USA
[3] eBay Inc, SJ, USA
{hungnguyen,shengshen,jexi,abagherjeiran}@ebay.com

Abstract. In the rapidly evolving landscape of digital information retrieval and online advertising, response predictor models have become indispensable tools for understanding user behavior and optimizing content delivery. These models aim to estimate the likelihood of a user response on a displayed item, such as a search result or advertisement, thereby enabling more efficient and targeted allocation strategies. However, the accuracy and reliability of response predictor models are significantly challenged by position bias – a phenomenon where the position of an item in a list influences the probability of user responding to it though either click, conversion, etc., independent of its relevance or quality.

This paper introduces a novel downsampling method designed to mitigate the effects of position bias while addressing the challenges posed by large-scale interaction data and resource constraints. Our approach preserves all positive samples and filters out a substantial amount of poor negative samples, maintaining the integrity of valuable information necessary for accurate predictions. By leveraging the insight that item response probabilities should be uniform across positions in the absence of bias, we propose a random filtering strategy that optimizes the preservation of valuable interaction data.

We demonstrate the effectiveness of our method through extensive offline and online experiments, showing that it not only complements existing bias mitigation techniques but also enhances model accuracy in resource-constrained environments. Our findings suggest that integrating this downsampling method with new training strategies leads to improved prediction performance.

Keywords: supervised learning · pointwise ranking · click prediction · position bias · e-commerce

A. Bagherjeiran et al. (Eds.): AdKDD 2025, CCIS 2796, pp. 42–56, 2026.
https://doi.org/10.1007/978-3-032-16358-5_4

1 Introduction

In the dynamic realm of digital information retrieval and online advertising, response prediction models [1–3,5,6,6,9–13,16,17] have become essential for deciphering user interactions and enhancing content delivery strategies. These models estimate the likelihood of a user engaging with an item – whether through a click, conversion, comment, or other feedback – enabling more precise and effective marketing decisions.

However, the presence of position bias – a tendency for items at the top of a list to receive more responses regardless of their actual relevance – poses a significant challenge to the accuracy and reliability of these models [5,13,17,17].

Position bias occurs primarily because users naturally focus on items at the top of a list, resulting in a higher response probability for these items compared to those further down [6,10]. This bias can distort the training data for response prediction models, causing the predictions to reflect patterns of user attention rather than the relevance of the true item. Therefore, addressing position bias is critical for improving the predictive accuracy and fairness of these models.

To counteract position bias, researchers have developed various techniques [5, 17]. Propensity scoring methods adjust click data by estimating the likelihood of clicks based on item position. Counterfactual learning frameworks infer click probabilities in scenarios devoid of position bias. Additionally, unbiased learning-to-rank algorithms incorporate position bias correction directly into the training process, enhancing the model's ability to generalize to unbiased click scenarios. Another research approach involves utilizing position information as a feature in modeling, or incorporating related data, such as the logit of the click-through rate for a position, into the training process via the base margin vector, which provides prior knowledge for model training [4].

High-quality response prediction models heavily rely on the user–item interaction data. The most valuable data includes positive samples (i.e. clicks or conversion) and good or high-quality negative samples (items seen but skipped and thus not clicked). The abundance of interaction data on popular recommender, search, and online advertising platforms poses a challenge, as resource constraints (e.g., limited RAM, CPU, GPU, or latency) make it difficult to process these large volumes. A practical solution is to randomly sample a sufficient training dataset from the raw data. However, this can result in the loss of valuable information, particularly positive and high-quality negative samples. This challenge motivates the search for solutions that preserve valuable information while allowing for smaller, resource-efficient training datasets. In this paper, we introduce a novel downsampling method that significantly reduces the size of the training dataset while preserving all positive samples and filtering out a substantial amount of weak negative samples (items displayed but not seen and not clicked, typically in lower slots), with minimal loss of valuable negative samples. This method effectively addresses position bias and complements existing techniques. We also propose several training strategies that yield slight improvements in model accuracy over current methods.

Our approach is based on the observation that, on platforms with a sufficient number of items, the top items displayed to users are generally of similar quality standard. In the absence of position bias, the click-through rates across all positions would be equal. Therefore, we aim to formulate a strategy for randomly filtering out negative samples to equalize the post-downsampling click-through rates across positions to that of position (let say) 1, which is not affected by position bias.

We present a range of experimental results to support our findings.

This paper is organized as follows: Sect. 2 reviews position bias models and existing mitigation approaches. Section 3 details our downsampling method. Section 4 introduces new training strategies based on our downsampling method. We present experimental results in Sect. 5 and conclude in Sect. 6.

2 Background

2.1 Setup

In response to a user visit or specific user query, online platforms surface a number of items to users, optimized for user engagement, thereby enhancing it's likelihood and optimizing the utilization of digital real estate. This real estate comprises of positions starting from first which typically gains the most traction [17].

The online platforms meticulously track user behavior, including metrics such as clicks and purchases, for subsequent analysis aimed at enhancing the user's shopping experience by showing the most relevant and impactful items on high valued positions. In the context of click prediction modeling for instance, researchers compile data on user clicks, along with associated user and item feature information, to construct predictive models. The objective is to leverage the comprehensive dataset to train the model, ensuring no critical information regarding user-item interactions is overlooked. Consequently, multi-position data is utilized in the training phase of the model. However, to evaluate the model's effectiveness, researchers may restrict the test dataset to data collected from positions that consistently capture user attention, regardless of the items displayed. Frequently, only data from position–1 may be considered as the test dataset.

2.2 Position Bias Model

We consider the following widely accepted model to address the position bias issue. The position bias model posits that the observed click, represented as a Bernoulli variable C, is contingent upon two latent Bernoulli variables: E and R. Here, E signifies the event where a user examines a document at a specific position k, while R denotes the event where a document d is relevant to a query q. The model is mathematically expressed as:

$$P(C = 1 \mid q, d, k) = P(E = 1 \mid k) \cdot P(R = 1 \mid q, d),$$

where $P(C = 1 \mid q, d, k)$ represents the probability of a click on document d displayed at position k given query q. $P(E = 1 \mid k)$ is the probability of examining position k, and $P(R = 1 \mid q, d)$ is the probability that document d is relevant to query q. This model assumes that examination is solely dependent on position, while relevance is dependent only on the query and document. For simplicity, we define the notations: $\theta_k = P(E = 1 \mid k)$ and $\gamma_{q,d} = P(R = 1 \mid q, d)$.

In scenarios where $E = 1$, the relevance R is fully observed through C. Conversely, when $E = 0$, C is invariably 0, leaving the relevance of the document unknown. A clicked document i indicates both examination and relevance.

In this study, the primary objective of multi-position click prediction modeling is to develop a model that can accurately predict the relevance of a given document (d) for a query q at position 1 (i.e. $k = 1$) with high accuracy based on the information of all collected clicks with users and documents features. using information from all collected clicks and user and document features. We outline some common approaches to tackle this challenge.

2.3 Naïve Approach

The most straightforward approach assumes that position bias is not a concern, meaning users examine all positions before deciding whether to click. In this scenario, $\theta_k = P(E = 1 \mid k)$ is always equal to 1 for every position. As a result, we train a click predictor model using all available training data points. However, this method may result in lower model accuracy because it does not account for the negative effects of position bias. In practice, the model tends to generate lower predicted click-through rates (CTR), represented as $\gamma_{q,d} = P(R = 1 \mid q, d)$, due to an inflated number of negative samples.

2.4 Position Information k as a Feature

In this approach [17], the position bias θ_k and relevancy $\gamma_{q,d}$ are not treated separately. Instead, complex models like XGBoost [4] are utilized to address the issue of position bias by incorporating position position (i.e. parameter k) as a feature alongside other user and item features. This allows the model to distinguish between clicks driven by content relevance and those influenced by positional prominence. By doing so, this approach mitigates bias, refines ad placement strategies, and enhances model interpretability by clarifying how position affects click probabilities. As a result, it leads to more accurate predictions and optimized advertising strategies.

2.5 Base Margin

In multi-position click prediction modeling, base margins in Gradient Boosting implementations such as XGBoost [4] serve as initial prediction scores that can incorporate prior knowledge, such as historical click-through rates (CTR) or outputs from other models. To tackle position bias via base margin, in practice we set it's value as the logit of position 1's CTR, i.e.

$$\text{logit}(p_k) = \log\left(\frac{p_k}{1 - p_k}\right),$$

where p_k is the k-th position CTR.

This initialization is crucial for capturing complex interdependencies between positions and adjusting for position biases, such as higher click probabilities for top positions. By setting appropriate base margins, the model can start closer to expected outcomes, enhancing convergence speed and accuracy. Specifically, for XGBoost, when used for classification tasks, typically optimizes a logistic loss function. Providing the base margin in log odds aligns with this loss function, potentially leading to better convergence and performance.

In practice, this approach outperforms using position information k as a feature because it does not rely on positions being in consecutive order. When positions are not sequential, the model's performance can suffer, whereas position-based margin information does not require strict positional correlation, thus maintaining effectiveness.

2.6 Expectation-Maximization (EM)

In [17], the authors introduce an innovative method utilizing the Expectation-Maximization (EM) algorithm to precisely estimate position bias, denoted as $\theta_k = P(E = 1 \mid k)$, and incorporate it into a multi-position click predictor model. The primary contribution of this work is the creation of an unbiased learning-to-rank framework that successfully distinguishes genuine relevance signals from position bias present in click data. By leveraging the EM algorithm, the model progressively enhances its estimations of both user preferences and position bias, thereby enabling more accurate ranking predictions.

The EM approach outlined in the paper requires a minimum of two training cycles (see *Algorithm* 1 Regression-based EM), with the outer cycle dedicated to EM and the inner cycle focused on comprehensive model training. Consequently, this method demands considerably more training effort compared to techniques based on base margin or position information (refer to Sect. 2.4). The paper illustrates that this method is less effective than those utilizing position information. Given its practicality limitations and lower effectiveness relative to position information-based methods, this approach is included here solely for the sake of completeness in the review.

Due to page constraints, we present two additional, less practical approaches in Appendix A.

3 Effective Position Debiasing Methods

3.1 Motivation

Typically, designers aim to capture all essential interactions between users and items in the training datasets, leading to the use of multi-position click predictor modeling despite position bias challenges. However, this objective becomes less feasible as the training data volume increases. Designers must allocate more resources, such as RAM, CPU, GPU, and time, to train the model, or alternatively, they may resort to randomly sampling a sufficient subset of the data if resources are constrained. Expanding training resources demands greater investment, which may not always be feasible. Consequently, random downsampling becomes a more practical and favored option, though it results in the loss of valuable interaction data between users and items, which is undesirable in many cases. This situation motivates us to develop a new training method capable of delivering strong modeling performance with a significantly smaller training dataset, while preserving all crucial information from the original dataset.

3.2 Key Idea

As discussed earlier, users are likely to skip ads displayed in lower positions, resulting in a large number of negative samples (i.e., samples with a click value of 0) that offer little insight into user-ad interaction. This prompts us to eliminate these negative samples. However, we lack an effective method to differentiate valuable negative samples (i.e., those skipped after user consideration) from the rest. Consequently, our best approach is to randomly select a sufficient number of negative samples, along with all positive samples (those with a click value of 1), to form the training dataset. Since downsampling is applied only to negative samples, all valuable positive samples are retained, given that the number of positive samples is significantly smaller than negative ones in online advertising datasets. This suggests that our approach to downsampling negative samples is optimal for preserving information.

Our proposed strategy for downsampling negative samples is based on the following assumptions:

Assumption 1 *Users consistently examine the ads displayed in position* 1. *In other words, position* 1 *is free from position bias.*

Assumption 1 is considered mild because users are naturally inclined to view ads in position 1 due to its prominent visual placement.

Assumption 2 *If all ads displayed across all positions are of average quality and there is no position bias, then the click-through rates for all positions are equal.*

Assumption 2 is more comprehensive than Assumption 1 because ads are ranked by their quality. However, it becomes more realistic when the number of ads far exceeds the number of available positions, and when the advertising platforms are well-known, attracting numerous high-quality, competitive advertisers. Additionally, Assumption 2 is more acceptable when ads are not ranked solely by relevance, such as in systems using generalized second price auctions [8], where ads are ranked based on a combination of their bid value b and their predicted click-through rate score $pCTR$, i.e. $pCTR \times b$.

These two assumptions lead us to randomly select a sufficient number of negative samples at each position so that, combined with their positive samples, the click-through rates (CTRs) for each position match the CTR of position 1. The following theorem outlines our proposed downsampling algorithm.

Theorem 1. *Let ρ_k represent the click-through rate of position k. For each negative sample at position k, if it is sampled with probability dr_k, where*

$$dr_k = \frac{\rho_k}{1-\rho_k} \times \frac{1-\rho_1}{\rho_1},$$

then all positions will have the same click-through rates, equal to ρ_1.

Proof. We consider position k and begin by initializing several key variables:

- a is set to the number of positive samples, which is equivalent to the number of clicks.
- b represents the number of remaining negative samples after sampling.
- c denotes the number of removed negative samples after sampling.
- The total number of negative samples n is defined as $n = b + c$.
- The total number of impressions i is calculated as $i = a + b + c = a + n$.

We first calculate number of remaining negative samples b based on the number of positive samples a and position-1 CTR ρ_1. Our goal is to make the CTR of position k after sampling equal to ρ_1 or we want to have $a/(a+b) = \rho_1$. This gives

$$b = \frac{a \cdot (1-\rho_1)}{\rho_1}.$$

The downsampling rate, dr_k, is calculated to adjust the distribution of negative samples relative to positive samples. The formula for dr_k is expressed in several equivalent forms:

$$\begin{aligned} dr_k &= \frac{b}{b+c} = \frac{b}{n} = \frac{b}{i-a}, \\ &= \frac{a}{i-a} \cdot \frac{1-\rho_1}{\rho_1} = \frac{a/i}{1-a/i} \cdot \frac{1-\rho_1}{\rho_1}, \\ &= \frac{\rho_k}{1-\rho_k} \cdot \frac{1-\rho_1}{\rho_1}. \end{aligned}$$

This rate aids in balancing the dataset by effectively reducing the impact of position bias, allowing the learning model to focus on more relevant data.

In practice, the position CTRs, denoted as ρ_ks, are calculated by randomly sampling a sufficient number of training data points. They are determined using the formula

$$\rho_k = \frac{\text{total number of clicks at position k}}{\text{total number of impressions at position k}}$$

.

Algorithm 1. Negative Downsampling Method

Require: Position CTRs ρ_k, $k = 1, \ldots, n$ and raw training dataset $\mathcal{D}$
Ensure: Training dataset $\mathcal{S}$

```
S ← empty set
for each data point d in the raw training dataset D do
  if d is a positive sample then
    S ← S ∪ {d}
  else
    if d is a negative sample then
      if d is at position k then
        R ← Random(0, 1)
        if R < dr_k then
          S ← S ∪ {d}
        end if
      end if
    end if
  end if
end for
```

This approach allows us to efficiently compute dr_ks values without needing to use the entire raw dataset.

Given a raw dataset $\mathcal{D}$, a downsampled training dataset $\mathcal{S}$, constructed using our proposed method, is outlined in Algorithm 1.

Initially, an empty training dataset $\mathcal{S}$ is established. We then proceed to examine each data point in the raw dataset $\mathcal{D}$ individually. According to Algorithm 1, if a data point is a positive sample at position k, it is added to the training dataset $\mathcal{S}$ with a probability of 1. If it is not a positive sample, it is included in $\mathcal{S}$ with a probability of dr_k.

Theorem 2. *Let ρ_1 and a_k represent the click-through rate of position 1 and the number of positive samples at position k. The number of data points in downsampled training dataset $\mathcal{S}$ after applying Algorithm 1 is equal to*

$$\frac{1}{\rho_1}(\sum_k a_k).$$

Proof. The proof is derived straightforward based on the proof of Theorem 1, i.e. the total number of data points in $\mathcal{S}$ is equal to the sum of all positive samples a_k and remaining negative samples b_k over all positions k and the fact $b_k = a_k \frac{1-\rho_1}{\rho_1}$.

In practice, due to the impact of position bias, the lower positions have a smaller number of positive samples. As a result, the number of data points in the training dataset $\mathcal{S}$ is significantly less than in the raw dataset $\mathcal{D}$.

4 Click Predictor Modeling with New Downsampling Method

In the previous section, we introduced a novel downsampling method specifically targeting negative samples. The primary objective of this method is to equalize the position CTRs across all positions to match that of position 1, thereby mitigating the negative effects of position bias. Once the downsampled training dataset $\mathcal{S}$ is obtained, we propose several new model training methods.

Table 1. Downsampling Rates dr_k for Different Positions

Position	1	2	3	4	5	6	7	8	9	10	11	12	13
dr_k	1.0	0.70	0.54	0.46	0.17	0.15	0.14	0.09	0.08	0.076	0.073	0.059	0.059

Position-independent downsampling (PID) This is the simplest approach, where we treat all data points as if they were sampled from position 1. This combined dataset serves as the training data for any existing training methods we prefer to use.

Position-dependent downsampling (PDD) This method is based on the observation that, after downsampling, while the position CTRs are equalized, the true CTRs of items at different positions are not necessarily equivalent. Items displayed in lower positions that receive clicks likely have a higher true CTR than those in higher positions. Therefore, we do not treat all data points as if they were sampled from position 1. Instead, we handle them separately to help models learn the true CTR of items more accurately. To achieve this, we incorporate the position information k as a feature.

5 Experiments

Table 2. Comparative analysis of performance models.

	AUC	Logloss	Bias
Ex. 1 (naïve training)	0.00000	0.00000	0.00000
Ex. 2 (base margin XGB)	0.01349	−0.00799	−0.67149
Ex. 3 (position k as a feature)	0.01547	−0.00855	−0.60399
Ex. 4 (PID)	0.01354	−0.00807	−0.65636
Ex. 5 (PDD)	0.01575	−0.00859	−0.60500

5.1 Datasets

We utilize datasets from a prominent online marketplace where hundreds of millions of buyers and sellers engage daily. This e-commerce platform offers an extensive array of products catering to a wide range of preferences and needs, along with programs that enable sellers to advertise their items. As a result, the platform must choose relevant ads or products from billions of possibilities to present to users. After identifying relevant items, they are ranked based on factors like click-through rate (CTR) and bid value. Developing effective click prediction models for item ranking is essential. The ranking process employs comprehensive user and item features for model training, with click values used as labels to build the click predictor. All user-item interactions are logged for system analysis, leading to a vast amount of data due to high levels of user and ad engagement. This creates opportunities for designers to craft robust click predictor models, but also introduces challenges, particularly in extracting valuable insights from data points with click values of 1 or from all positions, given constraints such as RAM, CPU, GPU, and time.

In our case, we gather *a dataset from two weeks of platform logs from an ads program* that details user and ad interactions, referred to as the raw dataset $\mathcal{D}$. We utilize a one-day log from position 1 as our testing dataset $\mathcal{T}$. The data points in $\mathcal{D}$ are derived from specific positions, with 13 positions considered for click predictor modeling. Each data point includes user and item features for training, with click values assigned as labels. Due to data publication restrictions at the e-commerce platform, the statistics are not published but they show that different positions exhibit varying behaviors.

5.2 Metrics and Offline Experiments

To measure the accuracy of click predictor models for a given test dataset, The Receiver Operating Characteristic curve (ROC Curve) [7] or ROC-AUC, Logloss [15] and Bias are in use. In the context of click prediction, bias metric quantifies the degree to which the predicted probabilities deviate from the observed click rates. Specifically, the metric is defined as follows.

$$\text{Bias} = \sum_{i=1}^{N} p_i / \sum_{i=1}^{N} y_i$$

where y_i is the actual label (0 or 1), p_i is the predicted probability, and N is the number of samples.

We study the impact of our new proposed negative downsampling methods to the click predictor modellings. It is important to note that our approach for click predictors can be directly applied to sale predictors. XGBoost models [4] are used as main models. We implement the following *offline* experiments.

- **Experiment 1**: The unaltered training dataset, $\mathcal{D}$, is used without incorporating position information k as a feature. This serves as the baseline for model performance evaluation.
- **Experiment 2**: Similar to Experiment 1, the dataset $\mathcal{D}$ is employed without position information k. However, position CTR logit values are utilized as base margin values, providing insight into the effectiveness of base margin XGB.

- **Experiment 3**: The dataset $\mathcal{D}$ is used with position information k included as a feature, assessing the performance of XGB when position information is considered.
- **Experiment 4**: The training dataset $\mathcal{D}$ undergoes downsampling using our proposed method, applying the dr_k as detailed in Table 1. Subsequently, position-independent downsampling (PID) is applied for modeling.
- **Experiment 5**: Similar to Experiment 4, the dataset $\mathcal{D}$ is downsampled using the dr_k in Table 1, but position-dependent downsampling (PDD) is employed, incorporating position information k as a feature.

The outcomes of all experiments are detailed in Table 2. Due to data publication restrictions of the platform, we have obfuscated the results by adjusting the performance metrics through subtraction of the values from Experiment 1 for each experiment. This approach offers a differential perspective on the performance variations across the experiments. Higher AUC values indicate better ranking algorithms, whereas lower logloss and bias metrics suggest improved ranking performance.

Note: Given the page constraints of the paper, we have elaborated on the significance of the improvements in AUC and Logloss in the Appendix, as they may seem minor due to the nature of the problem. B.

5.3 Online Tests

We carried out an AB test to demonstrate the effectiveness of our new downsampling method. Two XGB models were trained: one using the base margin method and the other with our new downsampling technique position-dependent downsampling (PDD). The base margin method is currently utilized because ads are displayed in non-continuous positions, making it the most practical solution for addressing position bias issues. The AB test spanned three weeks and consisted of two phases. In the first phase, data was collected over one week to build calibration for both models. The second phase ran for two weeks to compare the performance of the two models. The base margin XGB model served as the Control, while the downsampling-based XGB model was the Treatment. Both models received equal traffic during the AB test. Calibration of XGB model scores was necessary because we discovered that scores from the base margin XGB model were biased, despite the bias metric being favorable in offline experiments. We suspect this bias is due to the limitations of the base margin method in addressing position bias issues. To ensure the calibrated model scores of the base margin XGB model did not negatively impact system performance, we implemented calibration using the Isotonic Regression method [14]. The findings from the AB test, which assess the enhancement of the downsampling model compared to the base margin model, are presented in Table 3. Metrics such as ROC-AUC, Logloss, Bias, Click-Through Rate (CTR), Sale Through Rate (STR), and Gross Merchandise Bought (GMB) are included. A notable difference was observed between offline and online results. This discrepancy can be attributed to the conventional offline approach used in constructing XGB models, which may not fully account for the complex and dynamic nature of the entire e-commerce platform. Thus, this divergence is understandable.

Table 3. Relative Enhancement of Downsampling PDD XGB Model Compared to Base Margin XGB Model (95% Statistical Confidence)

AUC	Logloss	Bias	CTR	STR	GMB
+2.3%	−3.8%	+77.84%	+7.72%	+14.5%	+18.10%

A significant discovery highlighting the effectiveness of our novel downsampling method in tackling position bias is the bias metric of the model scores, which remains nearly optimal both before and after calibration due to our deliberate application of bias correction on the training dataset. Essentially, we enforce a constraint on bias within the training dataset. Before calibration, the scores are around 1.032, improving to 1.007 afterward, nearing the ideal bias metric. This is notably different from the base margin model scores, which are 1.337 before calibration and 1.035 after. In this method, we depend on an algorithm to address bias issues, but this algorithmic approach falters when encountering new, unseen items. Moreover, incorporating position k as a feature without the downsampling technique (as in Experiment 3) shows promising AUC improvements in offline analysis, yet it still faces bias challenges similar to those found in the base margin approach. Thus, by combining the new downsampling method with position k as a feature, we effectively alleviate position bias issues, as demonstrated by enhancements in both bias metrics and ranking performance, reflected through the ROC-AUC metric, in both offline and online environments.

6 Conclusion

This paper tackles the crucial issue of position bias in click predictor models. Our innovative downsampling method improves efficiency by reducing the training dataset size, preserving all positive samples, and eliminating many poor negative samples linked to position bias. This enhances training efficiency under resource constraints while retaining essential information for accurate model predictions.

Acknowledgments. GPT-4o is utilized to enhance the paper by rephrasing text and performing grammar checks throughout the document.

A Background

A.1 Randomization

A common approach to mitigating position bias in recommender systems is to randomly shuffle item positions for a small percentage of user traffic and train models exclusively on this data [9,16]. Implementations of this approach include complete shuffling, *RandTopN* where rank 1 and rank p are randomly swapped half the time [11], or *RandPair* where adjacent pairs are randomly shuffled [17]. While this method directly addresses position bias, it comes at a significant cost to the platform despite attempts at developing various strategies as it can negatively impact user experience and may conflict with allocation policies, such as those used in ad systems. Due to these limitations, we do not consider randomization a viable strategy for addressing position bias in this study.

A.2 Inverse Propensity Weighting

Addressing position bias can be achieved by incorporating position information during model training using inverse propensity weighting (IPW), which effectively shifts the data distribution toward a position-agnostic distribution [11,17]. Naive implementations in this approach use an item's position p as input and include: (1) absolute positioning: $w = 1 + p$, (2) log transformation: $w = \log(\beta + p)$, and (3) ratio-based weighting: $w = 1 - \frac{1}{\alpha + p}$, while more advanced approaches for IPW are discussed in Sect. 2.6. However, in our experiments, these strategies led to subpar model performance, and therefore, we do not report their results.

B Significance of Enhancing Model Performance

Although the improvements in AUC and Logloss observed in Table 2 may appear modest, they are of considerable practical importance due to the use of original, comprehensive datasets that are highly imbalanced with respect to clicks. Typically, non-click impressions vastly outnumber those with click values, often by a factor of 20 to 100, depending on the slot position. This imbalance necessitates substantial effort to accurately predict impressions with a click value of 1, making even slight gains in AUC and Logloss noteworthy.

To substantiate this point, we conducted three experiments under identical conditions, including the same training, validation, and test datasets, setup parameters, and feature sets. We trained three XGB models with depths of 5 (experiment 1), 10 (experiment 2), and 15 (experiment 3), each with 500 trees. The results of these experiments are detailed in Table 4. According to the design of XGB models, increasing the depth exponentially enhances the models' capacity, as evidenced by the increase in model sizes. However, the observed improvements in AUC, Logloss, and Bias remain relatively small. This is understandable given the complex nature of the datasets, as previously explained.

Table 4. Differences in performance metrics for model depths 10 and 15 compared to depth 5. The differences are calculated by subtracting the metrics of depth 5 from those of depths 10 and 15. A positive difference in AUC indicates improved performance, while a negative difference in Logloss and Bias suggests better performance.

Depth	AUC	Logloss	Bias	Model Size (Mb)
05	0.000000	0.000000	0.000000	1.9
10	0.000725	−0.000010	−0.007141	24.9
15	0.002273	−0.000233	−0.007849	112.0

References

1. Agarwal, A., Dudik, M., Wu, C., Langford, J., Schapire, R.E.: A general framework for counterfactual learning-to-rank. In: Proceedings of the 42nd International ACM SIGIR Conference on Research and Development in Information Retrieval, pp. 5–14 (2019)
2. Agarwal, A., Wang, X., Li, C., Wang, M., Bendersky, M., Najork, M.: Estimating position bias without intrusive interventions. In: Proceedings of the Twelfth ACM International Conference on Web Search and Data Mining, pp. 474–482 (2019)
3. Ai, Q., Guo, J., Croft, W.B.: Unbiased learning to rank with unbiased propensity estimation. In: Proceedings of the 41st International ACM SIGIR Conference on Research and Development in Information Retrieval, pp. 385–394 (2018)
4. Chen, T., Guestrin, C.: Xgboost: a scalable tree boosting system. In: Proceedings of the 22nd ACM SIGKDD International Conference on Knowledge Discovery and Data Mining, pp. 785–794 (2016)
5. Chuklin, A., Markov, I., De Rijke, M.: Click models for web search. Springer Nature (2022)
6. Craswell, N., Zoeter, O., Taylor, M., Ramsey, B.: An experimental comparison of click position-bias models. In: Proceedings of the 2008 International Conference on Web Search and Data Mining, pp. 87–94 (2008)
7. Duda, R.O., Hart, P.E., Stork, D.G.: Pattern Classification. Wiley-Interscience, 2nd edn. (2001)
8. Edelman, B., Ostrovsky, M., Schwarz, M.: Internet advertising and the generalized second-price auction: selling billions of dollars worth of keywords. Am. Econom. Rev. **97**(1), 242–259 (2007)
9. Hofmann, K., Schuth, A., Whiteson, S., de Rijke, M.: Reusing historical interaction data for faster online learning to rank for IR. In: Proceedings of the sixth ACM International Conference on Web search and Data Mining, pp. 183–192 (2013)
10. Joachims, T., Granka, L., Pan, B., Hembrooke, H., Gay, G.: Accurately interpreting clickthrough data as implicit feedback. In: Proceedings of the 28th annual international ACM SIGIR Conference on Research and Development in Information Retrieval, pp. 154–161 (2005)
11. Joachims, T., Swaminathan, A., de Rijke, M.: Unbiased learning-to-rank with biased feedback. In: Proceedings of the Tenth ACM International Conference on Web Search and Data Mining, pp. 781–789 (2017)
12. Liu, T.Y.: Learning to rank for information retrieval. In: Proceedings of the 2nd International Conference on Information and Knowledge Management, pp. 3–10 (2009)

13. Richardson, M., Dominowska, E., Ragno, R.: Predicting clicks: estimating the click-through rate for new ads. In: Proceedings of the 16th International Conference on World Wide Web, pp. 521–530 (2007)
14. Robertson, T.: Order restricted statistical inference (1988)
15. Shannon, C.E.: A mathematical theory of communication. Bell Syst. Tech. J. **27**(3), 379–423 (1948)
16. Wang, X., Bendersky, M., Metzler, D., Najork, M.: Learning to rank with selection bias in personal search. In: Proceedings of the 39th International ACM SIGIR conference on Research and Development in Information Retrieval, pp. 115–124 (2016)
17. Wang, X., Golbandi, N., Bendersky, M., Metzler, D., Najork, M.: Position bias estimation for unbiased learning to rank in personal search. In: Proceedings of the eleventh ACM International Conference on Web Search and Data Mining, pp. 610–618 (2018)

SIDE: Semantic ID Embedding for Effective Learning from Sequences

Dinesh Ramasamy, Shakti Kumar(✉), Chris Cadonic, Jiaxin Yang, Sohini Roychowdhury, Esam Abdel Rhman, and Srihari Reddy

Meta Platforms, Inc., Menlo Park, USA
{dineshr,shaktik,ccadonic,jiaxiny,sroychowdhury1,esam,sriharir}@meta.com

Abstract. Sequence-based recommendations models are driving the state-of-the-art for industrial ad-recommendation systems. Such systems typically deal with user histories or sequence lengths ranging in the order of $O(10^3)$ to $O(10^4)$ events. While adding embeddings at this scale is manageable in pre-trained models, incorporating them into real-time prediction models is challenging due to both storage and inference costs. To address this scaling challenge, we propose a novel approach that leverages vector quantization (VQ) to inject a compact *Semantic ID (SID)* as input to the recommendation models instead of a collection of embeddings. Our method builds on recent works of SIDs by introducing three key innovations: (i) a multi-task VQ-VAE framework, called *VQ fusion* that fuses multiple content embeddings and categorical predictions into a single Semantic ID; (ii) a parameter-free, highly granular SID-to-embedding conversion technique, called *SIDE*, that is validated with two content embedding collections, thereby eliminating the need for a large parameterized lookup table; and (iii) a novel quantization method called *Discrete-PCA* (DPCA) which generalizes and enhances residual quantization techniques. The proposed enhancements when applied to a large-scale industrial ads-recommendation system achieves 2.4× improvement in normalized entropy (NE) gain and 3× reduction in data footprint compared to traditional SID methods.

Keywords: Vector quantization · fusion · encoding · decoder · ads-ranking system

1 Introduction

Industrial ads-ranking systems incorporate diverse signals from multiple sources to accurately predict user-engagement towards specific content. Traditionally, these systems have relied on aggregation based signals, which summarize user behavior and ad-attributes into coarse grained features. However, this approach has limitations, as it fails to capture the nuances of user interactions over time. Recent works such as in [5–12] demonstrate the importance of long sequence user behavior for improvement in click-through-rate (CTR) prediction by leveraging $O(10^3)$ to $O(10^4)$ events. In such systems, there is a need to enrich user-engagement signals/events for improved prediction using content engagement

A. Bagherjeiran et al. (Eds.): AdKDD 2025, CCIS 2796, pp. 57–70, 2026.
https://doi.org/10.1007/978-3-032-16358-5_5

signals, which typically are in the form of embeddings. In this work, we address two major challenges while using quantized SIDs to enhance user-ad engagement predictions: (1) How can we perform VQ efficiently when we have a plethora of content signals (embeddings and categorical predictions) as is the case in industrial ads-ranking systems, and (2) How can we structure VQ outputs to utilize them efficiently along with improved ranking performance of downstream models? To address these questions, we propose a novel multi-input vector-quantized variational auto-encoder (VQ-VAE) (called *VQ fusion*), as shown in Fig. 1, which addresses the gap in existing SID approaches that require large volumes of data to relearn embeddings for different SID n-grams or *tokens*. The proposed *VQ fusion* method consists of an encoder-network that takes different content signals as input and produces a shared latent representation that is quantized and passed through a pseudo-symmetric decoder network; thereby enabling reconstruction of the different content signals. Thus, the proposed structured codebooks avoid relearning the ID-to-codeword mappings and significantly reduce the number of parameters and memory required in ads-ranking.

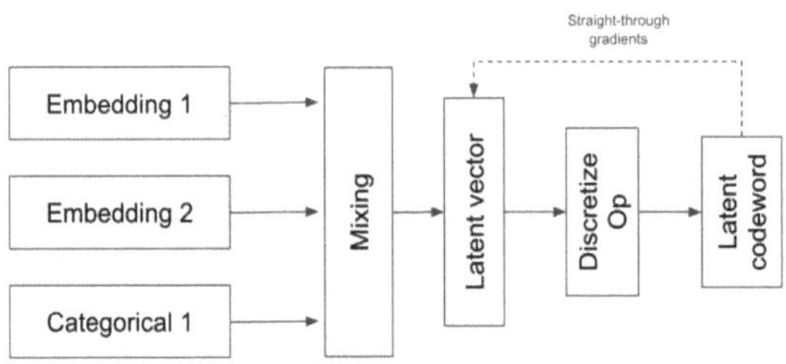

Fig. 1. The proposed fusion VQ-VAE setup (encoder portion). An unmixing decoder architecture (symmetric to mixing) is used to train the encoder.

This paper makes three major contributions. First, we propose a novel vector quantization method based on *Residual Quantization* called Discrete PCA (DPCA). Second, we detail a method for fusing multiple embedding and categorical signals into a single Semantic ID which we call VQ-fusion, thus drastically reducing the data storage cost. Third, we introduce a new usage of Finite Scalar Quantization (FSQ [11]) and the newly proposed DPCA methods to improve ranking outcomes using the so-called SIDE property, which stands for the ability to convert SIDs to latent embeddings in an embedding table free fashion. We demonstrate significant gains in ranking metrics (at least 2.4× gain in normalized entropy) and the total return on investment (at least 7.4× RoI) compared to existing approaches in an industrial ads-ranking setting.

2 Related Work

Scalar quantization [11] traditionally involves quantizing each dimension of a vector independently using a scalar codebook, which can be static (examples are `int4` and `float16` quantization which use 4 and 16 bits per dimension, respectively). A class of compression techniques involves finding a mapping to a lower dimensional subspace so that "most" of the information content in the embedding is preserved and the PCA method identifies the optimal linear mapping when the loss is euclidean. Vector quantization (VQ) started off with the now ubiquitous k-means clustering algorithm that can be extended in two orthogonal ways: (i) Residual k-means clustering which involves clustering the residuals to create a hierarchy of codewords and (ii) Product Quantization [6], which involves using parallel k-means algorithms on a subset of dimensions and is considered as a hybrid between scalar and vector quantization algorithms.

Another clustering technique is called Iterative-Quantization (ITQ, [4]). This involves using a linear transformation to map embeddings into the latent space where they are quantized using a binary $\{-1, 1\}$ codebook. Since the transformations are done in parallel (matrix multiplication), we classify this as a form of product quantization clubbed with auto-encoder methods. A similar auto-encoder with scalar (binary) quantization setup called Lookup-Free Quantizer (LFQ, [2]) was used recently for video generation. Others have proposed Finite Scalar Quantization (FSQ, [11]) which extends LFQ by allowing for more buckets per dimension. One can combine VQ based methods (e.g., k-means) with auto-encoder setup as presented in the paper on RQ-VAE [8] that improves RQ's ability to learn hierarchical structure by adding structured quantizer dropout, as is shown in the proposed work.

Recently there has been lot of interest in extreme scalar quantization for LLMs like 1.58-bit LLM [10]. We draw inspiration from this work and use a ternary $\{-1, 0, 1\}$ scalar codebok as a universal codebook for our proposed DPCA method. In terms of applications of VQ-techniques to ad-ranking systems like those presented in [3], the recent work on using RQ for defining SIDs [1] and the work on generative retrieval [13] stand out. Both these papers use n-grams of RQ codewords as SIDs and utilize these SIDs as categorical features, thereby relying largely on embedding tables. We use this approach and more traditional k-means as baselines in our experiments.

3 Vector Quantization Method

In this section, we define our proposed method *Discrete-PCA*, and expand on the techniques to combine multiple embeddings and categorical signals into one-feature via our proposed VQ-fusion method. Next, we demonstrate our embedding table-free technique called SIDE to convert codewords to embeddings in ads-ranking models. The base concept of residual quantization (RQ) [1] involves the use of D independent codebooks that are stacked on top of each other to compress the residue from the previous layer. The approximation to the original embedding is therefore the sum of the D selected codewords.

3.1 Structured-Quantization Method

We propose a new quantization technique by noting that k-means uses a single point for each codeword. This means that the codeword collection has no inherent structure. As a result we need a large number of parameters to represent the codewords (k times d) and we cannot increase the information content measured by $\log k$ significantly (except via product and residual quantization extensions of course). To circumvent this issue we make the codewords structured - to be precise we make groups of L codewords co-linear. Thus, the codebook has the following structure:

$$\mathcal{C} = \left\{ s_l \cdot \mathbf{u}_k + \mathbf{b}_k : \forall\ k, l \right\} \tag{1}$$

where $\mathbf{u}_k$ is the codeword group's direction vector (unit vector), $\mathbf{b}_k$ is the reference point for codeword group k and s_l is the signed distance of the selected codeword l from the reference point $\mathbf{b}_k$ along the direction $\mathbf{u}_k$; giving us our *Structured-Quantization* method.

Next, we present the inference logic that is leveraged by the training stage.

Inference Procedure. This three-step method identifies the codeword indices k and l given a codebook $\mathcal{C}$ and a point $\mathbf{x}$.

First, we first choose the "line" $\hat{k}$ which is closest to the given point $\mathbf{x}$ by measuring the distance of the point from the line corresponding the k-th codeword group and picking the closest line (by choosing $\mathbf{u}_k$):

$$\hat{k} = \arg\min_k \left(\|\mathbf{x} - \mathbf{b}_k\|^2 - |\langle \mathbf{x} - \mathbf{b}_k, \mathbf{u}_k \rangle|^2 \right). \tag{2}$$

Once we identify the closest line, we estimate the optimal signed distance $\hat{s}_{\hat{k}}$ through the following inner product:

$$\hat{s}_{\hat{k}} = \langle \mathbf{x} - \mathbf{b}_{\hat{k}}, \mathbf{u}_{\hat{k}} \rangle. \tag{3}$$

The estimated projection weight $\hat{s}_{\hat{k}}$ is then quantized using an scalar quantizer $Q(\cdot)$ with L bins to identify the codeword index $\hat{l}_{\hat{k}}$ for the signed distance. This scalar quantizer used is FSQ and is shared across the collection $\{\mathbf{u}_k\}$.

Training Procedure. For training this VQ-VAE model, in addition to the reconstruction loss, we add the commitment and codebook losses and use a straight-through estimator to propagate the gradients to the encoder network.

3.2 Towards Discrete-PCA

In this work, we assume that a vector codebook is redundant in the context of residual and/or product quantization based structured quantization; thereby setting the the number of vector codewords to 1. We design residual structured quantization as a form of *generalized PCA* due to its stacked nature which promotes the Matryoshka property [7] of such codebooks. Since the residual depth is difficult to increase due to its serial nature, we propose to use a combination of product and residual quantization to increase the quantizer bit-width. Additionally, we design the scalar codebook (s_l in (1)) by assuming that just three values $\{-1, 0, 1\}$ suffice for the signed distance. This follows recent research on Large Language Model weights, which suggest that such a ternary codebook can be universal for LLM weights [10]; thereby resulting in quantizer Discrete-PCA. The implementation of the scalar quantizer follows Finite Scalar Quantizer (FSQ) [11] with number of latent dimensions equal to 1 (or the number of product quantization groups when used in conjunction with PQ).

DPCA can be viewed as a form of generalized PCA where the projection weights can only take three values $\{-1, 0, 1\}$ and thus the *component vectors* no longer turn out to be orthogonal. The codebook collection of this method is given by the following expression:

$$\mathcal{C} = \sum_{d} \left(s_d \mathbf{u}_d + \mathbf{b}_d \right), \tag{4}$$

where d refers to the residual depth and s_d can take one of three values in $\{-1, 0, 1\}$. When used alongside product-quantization, we have p-parallel orthogonal codebooks, each with structure resembling (4).

3.3 SIDE: Converting SIDs to Embeddings

When codewords are exported, they are typically n-gram-ed to form a SID or a collection of SIDs. For instance, each codeword is of the form $\mathbf{c} \in \{-1, 0, 1\}^n$ and we convert these to Semantic ID (SID) using the following n-gram operation:

$$s = \sum_{k=1}^{n} 3^k (1 + c_k) \tag{5}$$

In the ranking model, this n-gram operation can be undone using floor divide and modulo operations that yields the codeword vectors $\mathbf{c}$ with entries in $\{-1, 0, 1\}$. These latent codewords are called SID Embeddings or *SIDE* and are used directly as embeddings. It is noteworthy that without SIDE, the memory requirement of any quantizer scales as $\mathrm{O}(\exp(Cb) \times d)$, where b is the number of bits and d is the dimension of the embedding for some constant C; due to embedding tables used for decoding embeddings. The proposed SIDE approach reduces this to $\mathrm{O}(b \times d)$ as shown in Fig. 2.

4 VQ Fusion

In this section we describe the ads-ranking systems that utilize a multitude of content signals. These signals can be broadly categorized into two types: embeddings and categorical predictions. While incorporating all content signals into an ads-ranking model can be challenging, adding each signal one by one using SIDs obtained from VQ-methods can lead to increased storage costs and

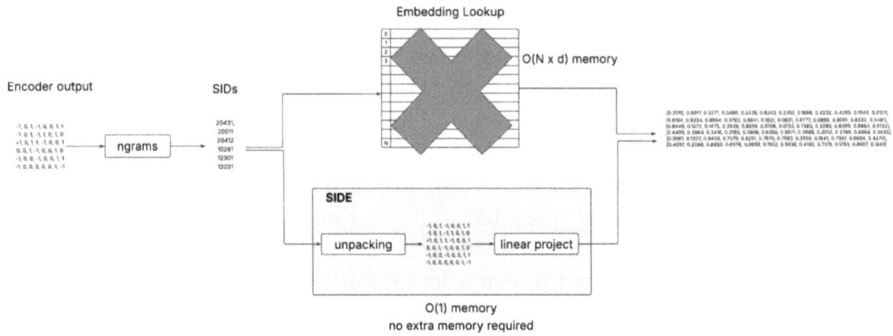

Fig. 2. Process of O(Nxd) memory removal using the embedding-free lookup in proposed SIDE. N = hash size of embedding tables and d=embedding dimension. The deterministic unpacking in SIDE ensures O(1) memory requirement.

decrease the overall system efficiency. To address this challenge, we propose a novel approach of fusion, called *VQ-fusion* that jointly encodes all available content signals (embeddings, categorical predictions, etc.) into a single SID. Our approach leverages the multi-input multi-output auto-encoder setup, where, the latent vector is learned using the following mixing model:

$$\mathbf{h} = f\left(e_1\left(\mathbf{x}_1\right), \ldots, e_n\left(\mathbf{x}_n\right)\right), \tag{6}$$

from the n input signals as $\{\mathbf{x}_k\}$. $e_k(\cdot)$ are the corresponding encoders for each input signal and $f(\cdot)$ is the fusion network. Next, vector quantization is performed $\mathbf{h}$ either using a version of FSQ [11] (with codewords for each dimension corresponding to $\{-1, 0, 1\}$) or our proposed DPCA method in Sect. 3 to arrive at the codeword $\hat{\mathbf{h}}$. Next, $\hat{\mathbf{h}}$ (via $\mathbf{s}$ demonstrated below) is used to reconstruct the inputs $\{\mathbf{x}_k\}$ using the decoder network. This network is trained end-to-end to minimize the reconstruction loss. To propagate gradients through the non-differentiable VQ operation, $\hat{\mathbf{h}}$ is replaced with its straight-through version $\mathbf{s} = \mathbf{h} - \texttt{stop\_gradient}\left(\mathbf{h} - \hat{\mathbf{h}}\right)$.

Next, we decode the inputs from the straight-through version $\mathbf{s}$ of the latent codeword using the decoder architecture which is symmetric to the encoder as $\hat{\mathbf{x}}_k = g_k\left(r\left(\mathbf{s}\right)\right)$, where $r(\cdot)$ is the shared model and $g_k(\cdot)$ are individual task decoders. By training this joint auto-encoder to minimize weighted reconstruction loss $\sum_k w_k \ell_k\left(\mathbf{x}_k, \hat{\mathbf{x}}_k\right)$ across all content signals, a compact and informative representation can be learned that leverages the underlying relationships between the different signals. This approach leads to reduction in the cost of the semantic ID representation and improvement in the quality of representations across signals.

5 Ads-Ranking System

In this section we focus on the relevant components of the ads-ranking stack [3] and highlight the changes needed to utilize the SIDE property of FSQ and

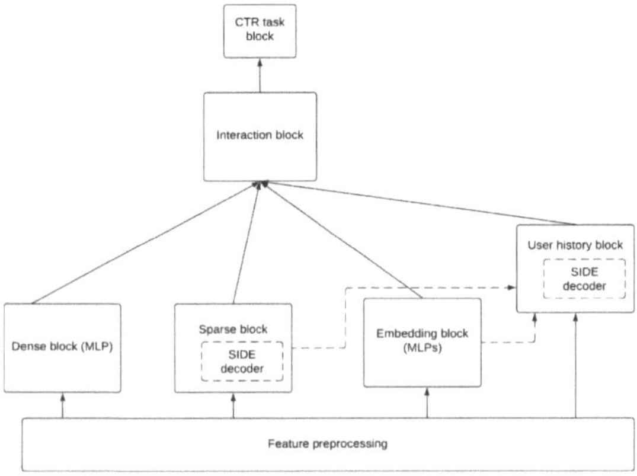

Fig. 3. Ranking system overview. The dotted lines represent query vectors for PMA that are typically drawn from Sparse and Embedding blocks.

DPCA based SIDs. Large scale deep-learning ranking systems can be broken down into (i) sparse (ii) dense (iii) embedding and (iv) sequence or user history blocks as shown in Fig. 3.

Sparse block: Each sparse/categorical/ID feature is mapped to a d-dimensional embedding $\mathbf{s}_k$ using a learnable embedding table $\mathbf{s}_k = S_k\mathbf{x}_k$, where, $\mathbf{x}_k$ is the r-hot representation of the k-th sparse feature and S_k is the associated embedding table for the feature.

Dense block: All dense features are collated and represented by a single vector $\mathbf{v}$. This vector is mapped to multiple d-dimensional representations $\{\mathbf{d}_1, \ldots, \mathbf{d}_r\}$ using learnable functions $D_k(\mathbf{v})$ for k in $\{1, \ldots, r\}$.

Embedding block: Embedding features are handled similar to dense features with each embedding being operated on by a separate function (typically a two-layer multi-layer perceptron) with $r = 1$ outputs to yield the d-dimensional representation for k-th embedding given by $\mathbf{e}_k$.

User history block: On the user-history side, the traditional approach is to convert timestamped sequence of sparse signals into embeddings using an embedding table and then leverage sequence algorithms like the Transformer-Encoder or Pooled-Multihead Attention (PMA) [9]. The user history block is a one-layer PMA module is $U = \text{softmax}\left(\frac{QK^T}{\sqrt{d}}\right)V$, where, U is a $k \times d$ matrix representing the k user history embeddings. Q is a $k \times d$ matrix derived from a subset of other sparse and embedding features $\{\mathbf{s}_k\}$ and $\{\mathbf{e}_k\}$. The key-matrix in PMA, $K = V\Theta$, where $V = [\mathbf{e}_1, \ldots, \mathbf{e}_l]$ is the $l \times d$ user history embedding matrix. Here l denotes the length of the user sequence and Θ is a $d \times d$ model weight matrix that maps each user history embedding to its corresponding key. We implement SIDs or their n-grams as sparse sequence features (based on prior work in [1]) to derive the user history embeddings $\mathbf{e}_k$.

In the following sections we demonstrate the application of the SIDE property in the user history block and compare the user-ad engagement results to that using SIDs (or their n-grams) directly as sparse sequence features. We convert the SIDs to embeddings $\mathbf{h}_k \in \mathbb{R}^t$ for some t typically smaller than d (as discussed in Sect. 3.3). Next, we use a d-dimensional projection $\mathbf{h}_k\Omega$ of these SIDE embeddings as features in the user history model, where Ω is a learnable weight matrix of shape $d \times t$.

5.1 Online Training

In this sub-section we present the online training components of the our VQ-fusion model (and correspondingly DPCA model) as a part of the ads-ranking system in production.

Data Collection and Model Training. The data collection process involves logging data from currently deployed upstream content models, which is then routed via logging to train our VQ-fusion encoders. The logged upstream data also serves as the ground-truth for training our auto-encoder. To ensure compliance with data privacy regulations, data is cleaned and filtered through rigorous privacy filters, such as ID masking, prior to any training. The VQ-fusion model converges quickly and needs 1 billion data points for initial offline training. Once the fusion model is trained, its inference is used to generate output features (SID) to train the downstream ranking model with 29 billion data points for the initial offline training.

Recurring Training and Inference. Upstream content models that produce embeddings leverage recurring training through periodic scheduled training jobs. We generate pipelines for our VQ-fusion model and apply them into the existing upstream training jobs. This results in our VQ-fusion models getting trained periodically whenever upstream models are trained. This also addresses any new item embeddings which are learnt in VQ-fusion during this recurring training. The inference output (namely SID) produces IDs that are then logged into downstream training tables and serve as output features for our ads-ranking system.

6 Experiments and Results

In this section, we present the results for reconstruction accuracy of the SID encoding methods RQ-VAE, FSQ and our proposed DPCA in multiple settings: (i) one-embedding at a time (1:1) for two content embeddings and (ii) in the context of VQ-fusion with the same two embeddings. Also, the impact of the proposed SIDE technique in capturing dot-product ordering of the two embedding collections in the 1:1 setting is presented. Finally we analyze the overall ads-ranking performances in Sect. 6.2.

6.1 Encoder Design

1:1 Encoder. We implement two content embeddings from the text-only content model (for converting text → embeddings) and the image-only content model (for converting image → embeddings). For both these embeddings we use 1 billion datapoints to train the 1:1 quantizers (text embedding quantizer and image embedding quantizer using each of RQ, FSQ and DPCA). For fusion setting we jointly train a single quantizer on the combined dataset of text and image embedding using FSQ, DPCA and RQ methods. The cosine reconstruction loss of each method is shown in Table 1.

Table 1. Cosine reconstruction loss comparison of three 24-bit VQ methods for two 1024-dimensional content embeddings. 1:1 refers to separate training of both the image and text quantizers while the fusion setting refers to using a single quantizer for both embeddings; thereby utilizing half the number of total bits. △ %age refers to the percentage increase in cosine reconstruction loss for fusion model for each method compared to 1:1 encoder model.

Setting	Method	Image	△ %age	Text	△ %age
1:1	RQ	0.1995	-	0.3066	-
	DPCA	0.1870	-	**0.2319**	-
	FSQ	**0.1549**	-	0.2435	-
Fusion	RQ	0.2224	11.47%	0.2892	5.67%
	DPCA	**0.1945**	**4.01%**	**0.2365**	**1.98%**
	FSQ	0.21607	39.48%	0.2803	15.11%

Parameter Tuning: We tune the 3 major hyper-parameters as the numbers of: scalar quantization buckets, residual quantization layers, and product quantization buckets, to minimize the reconstruction loss of the embeddings. This is performed by standard parameter sweep. Once the reconstruction loss is minimized, the selected parameters are used to test loss values of the derived SIDs in ads-ranking model as sparse features to ensure loss parity or improvements in ads-ranking model performances over raw embeddings.

VQ-Fusion. We train a single quantizer on the combined dataset of image and text embeddings jointly, thereby increasing the compression by a factor of two. In Table 1, Δ%age demonstrates the enhancement of the fusion process over 1:1 quantization method such that for image reconstruction tasks, 1:1 quantizer loss is 0.1995 and fusion quantizer loss is 0.2224 leading to Δ%age = 11.47%. We observe that in a fusion setting (joint training of both image and text quantizer), our proposed DPCA method has the least change in reconstruction loss when compared to FSQ and RQ methods as shown by the least Δ%age in Table 1.

Efficacy of Latent Codeword Representation. As discussed in Sect. 3.3, for FSQ and DPCA, the n-gram operation is reversed and centered (by subtracting 1 in this case) to convert the Semantic IDs into embeddings. Next, the following steps are performed for the 1:1 encoder: The kNN results (using cosine similarity) are computed for the 1:1 24-bit compression of the two 1024-dimensional content embeddings presented in Table 2. These kNN results are then compared to those obtained from the original raw embeddings' closest 20 kNN results (based on cosine similarity as well). We use Recall@k for different values of k to quantify the correctness of this comparison by using 1000 random seed queries picked from a 200K large embedding corpus.

Table 2. Comparison of DPCA and FSQ methods using Recall at 20, 50 and 100 for closest-20 neighbors as defined by the original embedding to show the efficacy of Semantic ID to latent embedding conversion (SIDE property).

Corpus	Method	R@20	R@50	R@100
Image	DPCA	0.1467	0.3326	0.5088
	FSQ	**0.2370**	**0.4187**	**0.5998**
Text	DPCA	**0.1703**	**0.3418**	**0.5213**
	FSQ	0.1323	0.2943	0.4848

Based on Table 2, we observe that both FSQ and proposed DPCA retain the dot-product ordering information present in the original embedding even with a massive $1024 \times 16 \div 24 \approx 682$ compression ratio. We verify these results qualitatively by inspecting k-NN results like those in Fig. 4.

Fig. 4. k-NN results with leftmost ad as the query using cosine similarity as the measure. Top: Thumbnails corresponding to original image embedding. Bottom: Thumbnails corresponding to 680x compressed FSQ SIDE representation. All of these ads are related to sneakers.

6.2 Ads-Ranking

In our ads-ranking systems, we predict two main tasks: click (CTR) and the conversion (CVR: eventual purchase) probabilities. In this paper we access the improvement for CTR prediction in terms of Normalized Entropy, which is defined as follows:

$$\mathrm{NE} = \frac{{}^{1}/_{N} \sum \left(y_i \log p_i + (1 - y_i) \log(1 - p_i)\right)}{\hat{p} \log \hat{p} + (1 - \hat{p}) \log (1 - \hat{p})}, \tag{7}$$

where, y_i are the labels, p_i are model predictions, $\hat{p} = \sum y_i/N$ is the prior probability and N is the number of samples. We utilize $\frac{(NE_{\mathrm{click}} + NE_{\mathrm{conv}})}{2C}$ to compute the overall RoI of the feature, where C is the logging cost of onboarding the feature.

In this experiment, we analyze the impact of adding K-means top-k clusters (k nearest neighbors) and SIDs as sparse-inputs (corresponding to the ad-item to be ranked) in Table 3 for a new content feature. Note that we use the same hash size for both K-means and SIDs. We now demonstrate the NE gains and RoI for a DPCA encoded feature used as an ad-feature in our ranking architecture.

Table 3. Incremental data and feature cost and normalized entropy gain relative to the baseline for a DPCA encoded ad feature. Baseline is a large-scale production ads-ranking model without the specific ad-features.

Method	k-means	SID
Incremental Cost	×1	×0.23
Click NE gain	**0.0108%**	0.0085%
Conversion NE gain	0.0037%	**0.0101%**
RoI	×1	×5.57

In Table 3, the cost C of features is directly proportional to the feature length used. k-means features with length 50 have cost $46.54kW$, while the SID features have length 3 and corresponding cost is $10.84kW$. This leads to a reduction in incremental feature cost by 76.7%. Hence from Table 3 we see that SID improves RoI by 5.57 times over traditional k-means method. This leads to an NE gain for using DPCA as 1.28X or 28%

Next, we present results for adding SID sparse inputs and SIDs recovered as latent embeddings (SIDE) for the user-history block in two settings: (i) 1:1 encoder (in Table 4) and VQ-fusion (in Table 5) for two different types of user history sequences.

In Table 4, we demonstrate the NE gains for using SID and unpacking it with SIDE for a DPCA encoded feature. The feature cost for SIDE is 1/3rd of SID since we just use a single n-gram from SID to unpack in SIDE. We observe that SIDE further improves NE gains over SID and enhances the RoI by 5.33× for

Table 4. Normalized entropy gain relative to the baseline for a DPCA encoded feature used as user history. Baseline is the large-scale production ads-ranking model.

Method	SID	SIDE
Incremental cost	×1	×0.33
Click NE gain	0.0082%	**0.0185%**
Conversion NE gain	0.0086%	**0.0111%**
RoI	×1	×5.33

the DPCA encoded feature on the user-side. Note that the hash size in SID is set to number of scalar quantization raised to power n-gram length, which is $64^3 =$ max cardinality of the SID feature, as shown in Sect. 6.2.

In Table 5, the gains from SIDE are further enhanced when by using a VQ-fusion SID feature comprising of 6 individual signals encoded into a single feature as. Here, the RoI improves by 7.40× over SID. This leads to an NE gain when using SIDE to be 2.44x or 144%.

Table 5. Normalized entropy gain for VQ fusion encoded feature comprising 6 individual signals, used as user history. Baseline = 6 different 1:1 encoded DPCA features used as SID.

Method	SID	SIDE
Incremental cost	×1	×0.33
Click NE gain	0.0100%	**0.0284%**
Conversion NE gain	0.0067%	**0.0124%**
RoI	×1	×7.40

Encoder Hyper-parameterization. From our ads-ranking experiments we demonstrate examples of varying the SID construction hyper-parameters and its impact in NE gains from the ads-ranking model. In the VQ-Fusion experiment, summarizing 6 user-side features in Table 5 and retaining the number of scalar quantization buckets as 64 and the number of residual quantization layers as 9 and increasing the n-gram size in SID, leads to the NE trend in Table 6.

Here, we observe that for SID, as more n-gram IDs are introduced (by making the prefix n-gram longer from 3 to 4) in the ads-ranking model, the NE gains reduce due to higher noise due to increase in hash collisions based on the embedding table size limitations. The maximum hash size for n-gram length 3 is $64^3 = 262,144$ and for length 4 is $64^4 = 16,777,216$. However, our proposed SIDE technique avoids hash collisions while unpacking the 4th n-gram ID leading to NE increase.

Table 6. Effect of prefix n-gram length on NE, keeping all other Encoder hyper-parameters fixed.

Prefix n-gram length	SID	SIDE
3	0.029%	0.044%
4	0.020%	0.046%

We also assess the effect of increasing the number of scalar quantizer code-words on the ads-ranking NE gains. Using 4 scalar quantizer codewords NE gain for SID and SIDE are 0.018% and 0.035% respectively. Extending this analysis to 64 codewords results in NE gains for SID and SIDE as 0.015% and 0.044%, respectively.

6.3 Discussion on Production Impact

In this section we assess the end-user benefits in terms of ads-score (values for both advertisers and users). Ads-score is the sum of the two entities: 1) ads-value or the value to advertisers calculated by adding paced-bids, 2) quality value which measures value to users, considering, positive interactions (e.g., clicks, likes), negative interactions (e.g., hiding an ad), ad-quality and user engagement. We observe overall gains of 0.17% ad-score with the launch bundle involving our proposed method (DPCA, VQ-fusion and SIDE put together) on the end-users.

In terms of other production metrics: our VQ-Fusion models deployed in online inference have very low latency ($<$ 500 ms) and memory consumption ($<=$ 2.5 GB), recurring training has 0.33% QPS regression. The inference model requires 2, 16GB T1 machines, leading to 20$\times$ lesser deployment machine costs when compared to traditional quantization models like k-means leading to improved RoI for our proposed system. The latency and throughput effect on feature logging due to the additional VQ-Fusion model is negligible, since real-time feature availability for ads-ranking systems remains less than 60 min SLA-bounds.

7 Conclusion and Future Work

In this paper, we have presented a novel approach to incorporating high-dimensional content embeddings into sequence-based recommendation models using vector quantization. Our method called VQ-fusion, which leverages a multi-task VQ-VAE fusion framework and an embedding table-free SID to embedding conversion technique (SIDE), has been shown to reduce storage costs while improving ranking outcomes on large-scale ads recommendation systems. The SIDE method can lead to significant improvements in the efficiency for the sequence learning paradigm in modern ad-recommendation systems.

Acknowledgments. The authors would like to thank our collaboration partners in meeting our deployment goals. For Deployment and Launch teams: Fan Xia, Doris Wang, Parshva Doshi, Mingwei Tang, Xinlong Liu, Leo Ding, Ahmed Agiza, Rahul Mayuranath, Dave Li. For Quantization support: Shuby Mao, Jijie Wei, Michael Chang. For Preproc support: Varun Bhadauria, Priya Ramani, Kapil Sharma, Tao Jia Sahaj Biyani. Package release: Pablo Ruiz, Fischer Bennetts, Hang Qi, Zhongjie Ma, Ying Xu. Infra and testing: Abdul Zainul Abedin, Zhaoyang Huang, Liang Tao. Management support: Kapil Gupta, Rostam Shirani, Arnold Overwijk.

References

1. et. al., A.S.: Better generalization with semantic ids: a case study in ranking for recommendations (2024)
2. et. al., L.Y.: Language model beats diffusion – tokenizer is key to visual generation (2024)
3. et. al., M.N.: Deep learning recommendation model for personalization and recommendation systems (2019). https://arxiv.org/abs/1906.00091
4. Gong, Y., Lazebnik, S., Gordo, A., Perronnin, F.: Iterative quantization: a procrustean approach to learning binary codes for large-scale image retrieval. IEEE Trans. Pattern Anal. Mach. Intell. **35**(12), 2916–2929 (Dec 2013). https://doi.org/10.1109/TPAMI.2012.193
5. Hou, R., et al.: Cross-domain lifelong sequential modeling for online click-through rate prediction. In: Proceedings of the 30th ACM SIGKDD Conference on Knowledge Discovery and Data Mining. **1**(1), 5116–5125 (2024)
6. Jégou, H., Douze, M., Schmid, C.: Product quantization for nearest neighbor search. IEEE Trans. Pattern Anal. Mach. Intell. **33**(1), 117–128 (2011). https://doi.org/10.1109/TPAMI.2010.57
7. Kusupati, A., et al.: Matryoshka representation learning (2024). https://arxiv.org/abs/2205.13147
8. Lee, D., Kim, C., Kim, S., Cho, M., Han, W.S.: Autoregressive image generation using residual quantization (2022)
9. Lee, J., Lee, Y., Kim, J., Kosiorek, A.R., Choi, S., Teh, Y.W.: Set transformer. CoRR **abs/1810.00825** (2018). http://arxiv.org/abs/1810.00825
10. Ma, S., et al.: The era of 1-bit LLMs: All large language models are in 1.58 bits (2024)
11. Mentzer, F., Minnen, D., Agustsson, E., Tschannen, M.: Finite scalar quantization: Vq-vae made simple (2023)
12. Pi, Q., et al.: Search-based user interest modeling with lifelong sequential behavior data for click-through rate prediction. In: Proceedings of the 29th ACM International Conference on Information & Knowledge Management, vol. 1(1), pp. 2685–2692 (2020)
13. Rajput, S., et al.: Recommender systems with generative retrieval (2023)

Profit Aware Ad Ranking with Relevance Constraint

Manavender Malgireddy[1(✉)], Dongyue Xie[2], Sergey Kolbin[1], Kurt Zimmer[3], Masoum Mosmer[2], and Patrick Phelps[3]

[1] Wayfair LLC, Seattle, WA 98103, USA
mmalgireddy@wayfair.com, skolbin@wayfair.com
[2] Wayfair LLC, Mountain View, CA 94041, USA
dxie@wayfair.com, mmosmer@wayfair.com
[3] Wayfair LLC, Boston, MA 02116, USA
kzimmer@wayfair.com, pphelps@wayfair.com

Abstract. Wayfair Sponsored Products (WSP) is a cost-per-click (CPC) advertising program aimed at improving product discovery and driving sales. At the heart of WSP is a ranking function that determines the placement of ads on a page. In this paper, we introduce a new ranking function derived from an optimization framework that maximizes overall profitability by jointly considering advertising revenue from clicks and profit from resulting sales. To maintain a positive customer experience, the formulation includes a relevance constraint. We evaluate the approach through offline simulations using counterfactual estimates of clicks and orders, analyzing the impact of different parameter settings on key metrics such as ad revenue, total profit, and estimated conversion rate (CVR). Finally, we share results from a successful online test, that validated the effectiveness of the proposed method, leading to its full deployment in production, and highlight key learnings from the study.

Keywords: Sponsored Products Advertising · Ranking Optimization · Profit Maximization · Revenue Maximization · Relevance Constraint · Profit-Relevance Tradeoff

1 Introduction

In recent years, e-commerce platforms have increasingly leveraged sponsored product advertising to enhance product visibility, boost customer engagement, and increase overall profitability [1,4]. WSP exemplifies this trend as a cost-per-click (CPC) advertising solution designed explicitly to facilitate product discovery and drive incremental sales on Wayfair's expansive marketplace. Central to the effectiveness of WSP is its underlying ranking function, responsible for determining the order of sponsored products shown to consumers.

This paper introduces a new ranking function developed as a solution to a carefully formulated optimization problem. Unlike, most traditional methods

A. Bagherjeiran et al. (Eds.): AdKDD 2025, CCIS 2796, pp. 71–84, 2026.
https://doi.org/10.1007/978-3-032-16358-5_6

that focus primarily on maximizing immediate advertising revenue from clicks [11], our proposed approach adopts a holistic view of profitability [10]. Specifically, it simultaneously optimizes for both advertising revenue generated through clicks and incremental profit derived from actual product sales. To ensure sustainable engagement and maintain user satisfaction, the optimization framework incorporates a relevance constraint, thereby safeguarding a positive customer experience and preventing irrelevant or overly aggressive advertising placements.

To evaluate and validate our proposed ranking function, we employed offline simulation methodologies leveraging counterfactual estimates of user clicks and purchase behavior. Through these simulations, we systematically explored the influence of different parameter settings on critical performance indicators such as advertising revenue, total profit, and estimated conversion rate (CVR). Our analysis delves deeply into understanding how the sensitivity of ranking positions responds to variations in profit-weighting and the strictness of relevance constraints. Additionally, we address the inherent challenges in striking an appropriate balance between maximizing profitability and preserving customer-centric relevance.

We also present results from an online test of our ranking function on Wayfair, highlighting key benefits and trade-offs of the proposed optimization approach, and providing insights for future improvements.

Our key Contributions are:

1. **Profit-Relevance Ranking Framework:** A novel ranking function derived from a constrained optimization problem that jointly optimizes total profit and relevance, supported by an efficient parameter optimization algorithm.
2. **Robust Constraint Selection Method:** The relevance constraint threshold is defined in terms of optimal expected conversion rate providing a robust and interpretable way to adapt the threshold to data/model drift
3. **Simulation-Based Analysis:** Analyze the trade-off between relevance threshold and key performance metrics through simulations, guiding threshold selection for deployment.
4. **Empirical Validation via Online A/B Testing:** Extensive online experiments validate the effectiveness of the proposed approach, demonstrating gains in both total profit and relevance metrics, as well as highlighting the contribution of the VCD (sales profit) component. Furthermore, the results highlight the critical role of calibration with respect to VCD.

2 Related Work

Most existing research on enhancing ad ranking focuses on improving click-through rate (CTR) models [1,2,4]. Yang et al. [9] have conducted an extensive survey of CTR prediction methods, particularly emphasizing modeling frameworks. More recently, Yan et al. [8] presented an architecture designed to ensemble various feature interaction modules. This architecture incorporates a depth selection controller, which dynamically determines the optimal layer for early exits, thus enhancing prediction accuracy. Additionally, another recent work [6] introduces a multi-task framework tailored for early-stage learning, effectively combining several final-stage ranking factors, such as ad clicks and ad-quality events. This approach has demonstrated improvements in overall ad recall and ranking consistency.

Revenue maximization represents another critical research direction for improving ad ranking. Approaches in this area broadly fall into two categories: i) integrating revenue signals during the training of underlying models, either through weighting or joint learning, and ii) directly using revenue metrics within the ranking formula. In the first category, authors in [7] introduced a framework that jointly models clicks and purchases to optimize sales revenue. Another approach, proposed in [12], involves independently training ranking models for relevance and revenue maximization and introduces a trade-off strategy using constrained optimization.

Our work aligns closely with the second category, wherein we propose a ranking function designed to maximize total profit while adhering to a relevance constraint. The most closely related study to ours is by Ge et al. [10], who introduced a scoring function that incorporates a weight balancing ad revenue against organic revenue. Their approach optimizes this balance per impression through grid search, subject to a constraint based on KL-divergence. Another relevant study [3] introduces distinct weights for ad revenue and advertiser ROI, tuning these weights through split testing with equally-sized buckets. They employ an online learning approach following an epsilon-first strategy, beginning with pure exploration and subsequently transitioning to pure exploitation.

3 Proposed Approach

3.1 Optimization Problem

Our objective is to maximize the expected total profit while enforcing a relevance constraint to ensure a high-quality customer experience. We formulate this objective as a constrained optimization problem, whose solution yields a scoring function used to rank ads. To proceed, we first define the following key terms that will support the formulation of this optimization problem.

Decision variables: Let $x_{rs} = 1$ indicate that the SKU (Product) s is selected to be shown as an impression for request r; otherwise $x_{rs} = 0$. The full set of decision variables is defined as:

$$x = \{x_{rs} \in \{0, 1\} : r \in R, s \in S_r\} \tag{1}$$

Expected Total Profit: Captures the expected profit from both ad clicks and product sales:

$$\begin{aligned} eTotalProfit(x) = \sum_{r \in R} \sum_{s \in S_r} \Big(&(pClick_{rs} \cdot bid_s) + \\ &W_1 (pPurchase_{rs} \cdot VCD_{rs}) \Big) x_{rs}, \end{aligned} \tag{2}$$

We assume access to $pClick_{rs}$, $pPurchase_{rs}$, and VCD_{rs} as given inputs derived from upstream machine learning models. The details of these models are beyond the scope of this paper.
where:

- $pClick_{rs}$: Probability of user clicking on a SKU s for request r
- $pPurchase_{rs}$: Probability of user purchasing SKU s for request r
- VCD_{rs}: Predicted variable contribution dollar on SKU s for request r. Sales profit term used in our objective.
- bid_s: Advertiser bid for SKU s
- $W_1 \in [0,1]$: Weight assigned to profit from sales

Expected Conversion Rate:

$$eCVR(x) = \frac{\sum_{r \in R} \sum_{s \in S_r} pPurchase_{rs} \cdot x_{rs}}{\sum_{r \in R} \sum_{s \in S_r} x_{rs}} \tag{3}$$

Optimization Problem The goal is to maximize expected total profit while maintaining a minimum threshold of relevance, enforced through a constraint on expected conversion rate:

$$\begin{aligned} &\max_x eTotalProfit(x) \\ s.t.\ \ &eCVR(x) \geq b_0, \end{aligned} \tag{4}$$

where b_0 is a lower bound on expected conversion rate, used as a relevance constraint to help preserve user experience and engagement.

3.2 Scoring Function

We solve the optimization problem in Equation (4) by converting it into a dual problem using the Lagrangian method. The Lagrangian function after regrouping the terms involving x_{rs} is defined as:

$$\begin{aligned} L(x, \lambda) = \sum_{r \in R} \sum_{s \in S_r} \Big[&(pClick_{rs} \cdot bid_s) + W_1 \cdot (pPurchase_{rs} \cdot VCD_{rs}) \\ &+ \lambda_0 \cdot pPurchase_{rs} - \lambda_0 \cdot b_0 \Big] x_{rs} \end{aligned} \tag{5}$$

Here, λ_0 is the Lagrange multiplier associated with the relevance constraint, which enforces a minimum expected conversion rate (eCVR$(x) \geq b_0$). This term reflects the marginal value of satisfying the constraint: a higher value of λ_0 increases the importance of purchase probability in the ranking function, encouraging the selection of more relevant SKUs.

The Lagrangian dual function is defined as:

$$F(\lambda) = \max_x L(x, \lambda) \tag{6}$$

and the corresponding dual optimization problem is:

$$\begin{aligned} &\min_{\lambda} F(\lambda) \\ s.t.\ \ &\lambda_0 \geq 0 \end{aligned} \tag{7}$$

Let us denote the expression inside the summation of equation (5) as the scoring function:

$$\begin{aligned} Score(r,s) =&(pClick_{rs} \cdot bid_s) + W_1(pPurchase_{rs} \cdot VCD_{rs}) \\ &+ \lambda_0 \cdot pPurchase_{rs} - \lambda_0 \cdot b_0 \end{aligned} \tag{8}$$

We observe that, for a given value of λ_0, the optimal solution to Equation (6) is obtained by setting:

$$x_{rs} = \begin{cases} 1, & \text{if } Score(r,s) > 0 \\ 0, & \text{otherwise} \end{cases} \tag{9}$$

If we add a constraint—such as selecting exactly 12 items per request—the solution is to sort the SKUs by their scoring values and choose the top 12. More generally, solving Equation (6) involves ranking SKUs in descending order of their scores and selecting the desired number to show as impressions.

Since the term $\lambda_0 \cdot b_0$ is constant across all SKUs for a given request, it doesn't affect their ranking. We can safely remove it from the scoring function to simplify computation. The resulting scoring function is:

$$\begin{aligned} Score(r,s) =&(pClick_{rs} \cdot bid_s) + W_1(pPurchase_{rs} \cdot VCD_{rs}) \\ &+ \lambda_0 \cdot pPurchase_{rs} \end{aligned} \tag{10}$$

This scoring function offers a practical and interpretable approach to ranking SKUs by jointly considering ad revenue, purchase-driven profit, and relevance. The term $\lambda_0 \cdot pPurchase_{rs}$ serves as a relevance incentive, promoting SKUs with higher purchase likelihood. Tuning λ_0 allows control over the trade-off between monetization (through ad revenue and sales profit) and relevance (via estimated conversion rate).

3.3 Policy for Picking Threshold b_0

The threshold b_0 in equation (4) represents the target average pPurchase value we aim to achieve from the displayed SKUs. To simplify the optimization process, we compute this average using only the top 12 SKUs per page request, as these typically account for the vast majority of ad impressions.

Determining an absolute value for b_0 based on historical data is challenging due to variability in user behavior, changes in the pPurchase model, and other dynamic factors. Instead, we define b_0 relative to the optimal expected conversion rate, ensuring consistency even as the model or data evolves:

$$b_0 = \alpha \cdot eCVR^* \tag{11}$$

Here, $\alpha \in [0, 1]$ is a tunable parameter representing the desired proportion of the optimal performance.

$eCVR^*$ denotes the maximum achievable expected conversion rate, obtained by ranking SKUs purely by their predicted pPurchase values.

For instance, setting $\alpha = 0.90$ implies a deliberate choice to target at least 90% of the optimal $eCVR$. This allows for a controlled trade-off, enabling other priorities such as business objectives, user experience, or content diversity.

This formulation using α enhances interpretability and maintains stability across shifts in data distribution or model updates, while providing flexibility to adapt b_0 over time.

3.4 Solving for λ_0

We utilize historical auction data that includes all candidate SKUs considered in each auction, along with their associated scores—such as *pClick*, *pPurchase*, and *VCD*. For a given value of α, we first compute the corresponding threshold b_0 as described in Sect. 3.3. We then apply the iterative search procedure outlined in Algorithm 1 to identify the optimal value of λ_0 for the specified W_1 and b_0. Figure 1 illustrates the convergence behavior of the dual and primal objectives, as well as the progression of the λ_0 values during optimization.

Algorithm 1: Iterative Dual Solver

Input: W_1, b_0, step size μ, iter threshold m, tol., λ
Output: λ, p_{best}, d_{best}

$\lambda \leftarrow 10^6$, $i, t \leftarrow 0$, $d_{\text{best}} \leftarrow \infty$, $p_{\text{best}} \leftarrow -\infty$;
repeat
  Solve Eq. 8 for solution x, dual d, primal p;
  if *constraint violated* **then**
    $\lambda \leftarrow \lambda + \lambda\mu$;
  else
    $\lambda \leftarrow \lambda - \lambda\mu$;
  end
  if $d < d_{best}$ **then**
    $d_{\text{best}} \leftarrow d$, $t \leftarrow 0$;
  else
    $t \leftarrow t + 1$;
  end
  $i \leftarrow i + 1$;
  if $t \geq m$ **then**
    $\mu \leftarrow \mu/2$, $t \leftarrow 0$;
  end
until $|p_{best} - d_{best}| \leq tol.$;

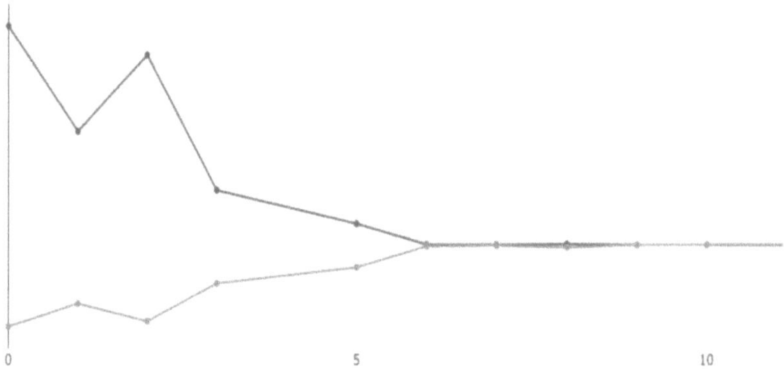

(a) Convergence of Objectives: The Y-axis represents objective values, while the X-axis indicates iterations. The blue line (top) corresponds to the dual objective, and the orange line (bottom) represents the primal objective.

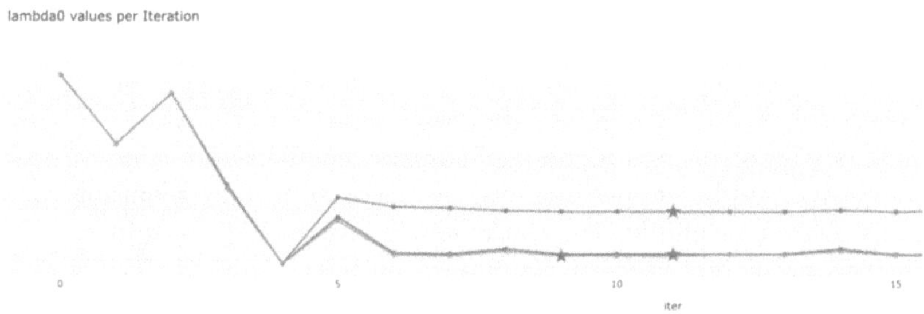

(b) Lambda Convergence: The Y-axis shows lambda values, and the X-axis represents iterations. Each line corresponds to a different platform (Web, MWeb, MApp), with a star indicating the optimal value.

Fig. 1. Convergence plots for objectives and lambda.

4 Offline Simulations

Before any online testing or deployment, we conduct offline simulations to select the optimal combination of parameters $\{W_1, \lambda_0\}$ in the scoring formula (10). These simulations serve as a critical step in understanding the impact of model parameters before deploying changes in a live environment.

The motivation for offline simulation is twofold: first, to simulate SKU rankings within each auction in order to analyze ranking shifts, SKU dynamics, as well as the ads competitiveness; and second, to validate that the proposed ranking method improves key business metrics, such as total profit and advertising revenue, without sacrificing user experience and business value. By leveraging counterfactual estimates of user clicks and purchases, we can approximate real-world outcomes across a range of parameter settings, enabling a deeper understanding of model sensitivity and trade-offs.

In this section, we describe the overall simulation methodology and highlight the metrics used to guide decision-making ahead of production rollout.

4.1 Approach

The offline simulation workflow consists of the following key steps:

1. **Collect** logged auction data from production,
2. **Re-rank** products using proposed parameter configurations and ranking method,
3. **Compute** simulation metrics, and
4. **Compare** results across different settings of the ranking function.

As discussed in the previous section, the value of the Lagrange multiplier λ_0 is determined by solving an optimization problem given a target relative conversion constraint α. For each parameter pair $\{W_1, \alpha\}$, we solve for λ_0, compute a ranking score for each product and sort SKUs in descending order of that score.

In practice, we choose W_1 values using a fixed grid ranging from 0 to 1, typically in steps of 0.01. The α values are chosen relative to the baseline "business-as-usual" (BAU) or in-production configuration. Usually the values are higher than the BAU level but upper bounded by 1. For all metrics requiring counterfactual estimates, we employ the methodology proposed by Nguyen et al. [5].

To comprehensively evaluate the impact of different parameter settings, we examine a range of metrics. Some of them are based on directly observable data, and others estimated through counterfactual modeling. Below, we group these into two these categories:

System-Driven Metrics:

- **Display Price**: The average listed price of products shown in ranked results.
- **Ratings and Review Count**: Aggregated indicators of product quality and popularity.
- **Bid Sensitivity**: Defined as the average change in a SKU's ranking position when its bid is increased by 50%. This metric captures how responsive the system is to bid adjustments. Higher sensitivity indicates a bid-driven system, while lower sensitivity suggests the ranking is more influenced by relevance or profitability factors.

Customer Interaction Metrics:

- **Ad Revenue**: Profit contribution from ad-driven clicks.
- **WSP Product VCD**: Profit from purchases attributed to ad impressions.
- **Total VCD**: Sum of Ad Revenue and WSP Product VCD.
- **ROAS**: Return on ad spend, defined as the ratio of ad revenue to ad cost.
- **CPC**: Cost per click.

- **CTR**: Click-through rate defined as ratio of clicks to impressions.
- **CVR**: Conversion rates defined as ratio of attributed orders to impressions

This structured evaluation allows for systematic tuning of ranking parameters and a better understanding of their impact on profitability, customer experience, and advertiser value.

4.2 Numerical Examples

We show the simulation results on auctions from customer search pages. In Fig. 2, we present the relative changes in key business metrics compared to the baseline (BAU) configuration. The results correspond to a fixed W_1 value, with the x-axis representing the α value used in the optimization, and the y-axis indicating metric lifts.

As α increases, the Lagrange multiplier λ_0 increases accordingly, reflecting stronger enforcement of the relevance constraint. Total VCD and ROAS both rise sharply beyond $\alpha \approx 0.7$, while ad profit from clicks starts to decline. This outcome suggests a trade-off between product-related profit and advertising revenue.

CTR and CVR also improve as α increases, especially when $\alpha > 0.7$, which indicates that user engagement benefits from more relevant product rankings. At the same time, CPC drops significantly with larger α values. This reduction is due to the decreasing influence of the bidding component in the ranking score. Bid sensitivity also declines, since the ranking becomes less responsive to changes in bids when relevance dominates the scoring logic.

Although CTR increases, it does not fully compensate for the decline in CPC. As a result, ad profit continues to fall as α grows. Display price also trends downward at higher α values. This is consistent with customer preference for more affordable products, which the relevance-focused ranking tends to prioritize.

Overall, these results underscore a fundamental trade-off between profitability and relevance. Tuning the α parameter provides a practical way to manage this balance and align the ranking strategy with specific business objectives.

Based on simulation results, we selected two variants for online testing. One variant employed conservative parameter values for weight W_1 and α, while the other used more aggressive settings to effectively gauge performance differences. Table 1 summarizes the simulation outcomes for both variants. Subsequently, we'll compare these simulation results to the online test findings in Table 2, highlighting how effectively the simulations guided our choice of variants for testing.

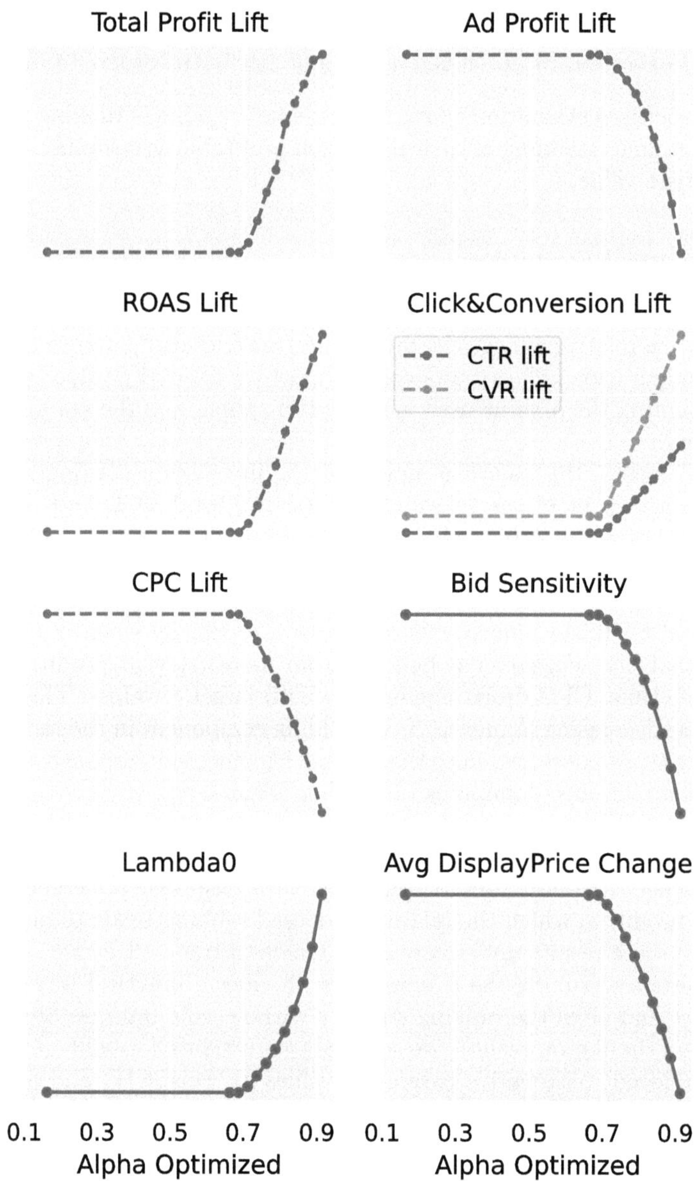

Fig. 2. Simulation results for fixed W_1: X-axis shows optimization parameter α, Y-axis shows relative metric changes vs. BAU. Last three plots (Lambda0, bid sensitivity, price change) are *system-driven metrics.*

Table 1. Simulation Results % lifts vs BAU.

Metric	Sim V1 (Conservative)	Sim V2 (Aggressive)
CTR	13.2	22.5
CVR	31.4	51.6
Total VCD	20.5	32.9
Ad Revenue	0.2	−7.7
ROAS	32.9	71.6
CPC	−11.4	−24.7
Display Price	4.8	36.7

5 Online Experiments

Table 2. Online A/B test results % lifts vs BAU. All numbers are statistically significant at 10%

Metric	V1 (Conservative)	V2 (Aggressive)
CTR	13.4	24.1
CVR	22.8	37.7
3 Total VCD	14.3	24.8
Ad Revneue	1.3	−5.0
ROAS	23.4	42.8
CPC	−10.3	−23.3
Display Price	5.9	29.1

The baseline (BAU) model for comparison uses the ranking formula $pPurchase * maxBid$. In contrast, the test variants utilize the equation described in Equation (8), each with distinct settings for W_1 and λ_0. We conducted the test for four weeks; Table 2 summarizes the results, indicating that both variants demonstrated overall positive outcomes.

Both test variants resulted in positive Total VCD, with the aggressive variant achieving a higher lift overall. However, despite its higher Total VCD, the aggressive variant showed negative Ad VCD due to a decline in CPC. This occurred because it assigns greater weight to relevance ($pPurchase$), promoting relevant products even if they have lower bids. Additionally, the aggressive variant caused a significant increase in display prices due to the higher emphasis on W1. Considering these factors, we opted to launch the conservative variant to maintain a balance between Ad VCD and Total VCD, and to minimize the customer impact associated with higher prices.

We now compare the results of the offline simulation with the outcomes of the online experiment. As shown in Tables 1 and 2, the simulation results directionally match the real A/B test outcomes across key metrics. Notably, trends in CTR, Ad VCD, CPC, and Display Price align closely, reinforcing the reliability of the simulation framework. Although other metrics exhibit minor deviations, they remain directionally consistent. These differences are expected because simulations exclusively focus on WSP products, whereas live pages incorporate organic listings, promotional banners, and other dynamic content. Moreover, metrics related to orders naturally exhibit higher variance, introducing additional noise into the simulation results. Overall, the observed consistency supports the use of offline simulations as a dependable proxy for assessing ranking impacts prior to online deployment.

5.1 VCD Sensitivity Test

In the previous test, each of the two variants differed in both the W_1 and λ_0 values, making it difficult to isolate the effect of the VCD term. To address this, we conducted a follow-up test where the control was the previously promoted variant (with both W_1 and λ_0 terms), and the test variant had W_1 set to 0. The results show a 2.9% drop in total VCD (Table 3), with all other ad metrics remaining neutral. This indicates that including the VCD term contributes to increased overall profit, aligning with the intended outcome of the proposed ranking.

Table 3. VCD Sensitivty Test % Lifts vs BAU. Bold = significance at 10%

Metrics	No-VCD
CTR	−0.88
CVR	0.90
Total VCD	**−2.94**
Ad Revenue	−0.31
ROAS	0.05
CPC	0.0

5.2 Learnings from an Expansion Test

Following a successful launch in the US, we expanded the online test to the UK using the same methodology. However, we saw unexpected drops in key metrics like CTR and CVR. These declines are typically linked to either poor model calibration or a low α_0 value. We verified that overall calibration quality was good, and the treatment's α_0 was actually higher than the control, which should have improved CVR.

Further analysis revealed poor **CVR calibration with respect to VCD** (Fig. 3a). Higher VCD values led to inflated *pPurchase* scores, causing high-priced SKUs to be ranked higher despite lower actual conversion rates. This misalignment explained the metric declines.

As a short-term fix, we applied a simple transformation to the *pPurchase* scores:

$$pPurchase' = c \cdot \frac{pPurchase}{(VCD + a)^b}$$

where a, b, c are tunable parameters. This adjustment led to an improved calibration (Fig. 3b) and yielded better results in the simulations. We are currently in the process of re-running the online experiment in UK.

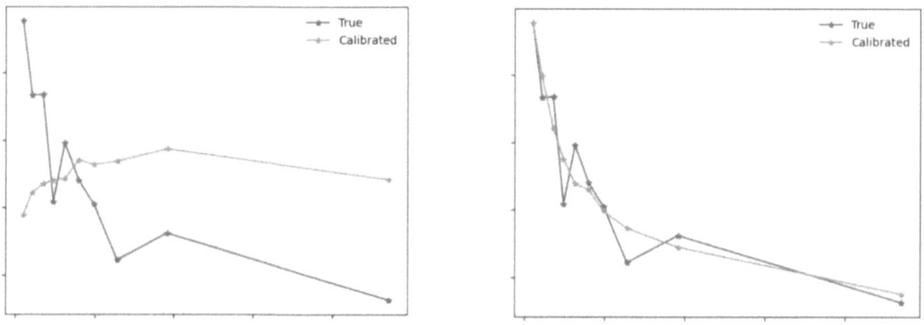

(a) Before Transformation

(b) After Transformation

Fig. 3. Calibration of pPurchase w.r.t VCD. X-axis is VCD bins and Y-axis is CVR.

6 Conclusion and Future Work

We introduced a new ad ranking function designed to maximize total profit while maintaining a balance with relevance. To support this, we proposed an elegant method for abstracting the relevance constraint using a more interpretable and robust parameter α_0. Through extensive simulations, we demonstrated how key performance metrics respond to variations in α_0 providing actionable guidance for selecting effective values in online experimentation. The approach delivered a 14% increase in total profit and a 22% improvement in CVR compared to the business-as-usual (BAU) baseline.

Moreover, insights from an expansion experiment highlighted the necessity for accurately calibrated pPurchase scores relative to VCD, underscoring calibration as a critical factor for the effectiveness of our proposed approach.

Future research directions include applying relevance constraints at finer granularities, such as individual queries or product classes, recognizing that different query intents and item categories may exhibit distinct user behaviors and varying trade-offs between relevance and profitability.

References

1. Cheng, H.T., et al.: Wide & deep learning for recommender systems. In: Proceedings of the 1st Workshop on Deep Learning for Recommender Systems, pp. 7–10. DLRS 2016, Association for Computing Machinery, New York, NY, USA (2016). https://doi.org/10.1145/2988450.2988454
2. He, X., et al.: Practical lessons from predicting clicks on ads at facebook. In: Proceedings of the Eighth International Workshop on Data Mining for Online Advertising, pp. 1–9. ADKDD'14, Association for Computing Machinery, New York, NY, USA (2014). https://doi.org/10.1145/2648584.2648589
3. Levi, O.: Online learning of a ranking formula for revenue and advertiser ROI optimization. In: Ferro, N., Lucchese, C., Maistro, M., Perego, R. (eds.) Proceedings of the 1st International Workshop on LEARning Next gEneration Rankers co-located with the 3rd ACM International Conference on the Theory of Information Retrieval (ICTIR 2017), Amsterdam, The Netherlands, October 1, 2017. CEUR Workshop Proceedings, vol. 2007. CEUR-WS.org (2017). https://ceur-ws.org/Vol-2007/LEARNER2017_full_1.pdf
4. McMahan, H.B., et al.: Ad click prediction: a view from the trenches. In: Proceedings of the 19th ACM SIGKDD International Conference on Knowledge Discovery and Data Mining, pp. 1222–1230. KDD '13, Association for Computing Machinery, New York, NY, USA (2013). https://doi.org/10.1145/2487575.2488200
5. Nguyen, P.H., Gligorijevic, D., Borah, A., Adalinge, G., Bagherjeiran, A.: Practical budget pacing algorithms and simulation test bed for ebay marketplace sponsored search
6. Wang, X., et al.: Towards the better ranking consistency: a multi-task learning framework for early stage ads ranking (2023). https://arxiv.org/abs/2307.11096
7. Wu, L., Hu, D., Hong, L., Liu, H.: Turning clicks into purchases: revenue optimization for product search in e-commerce. In: The 41st International ACM SIGIR Conference on Research & Development in Information Retrieval, pp. 365–374. SIGIR '18, Association for Computing Machinery, New York, NY, USA (2018). https://doi.org/10.1145/3209978.3209993
8. Yan, Y., Li, L.: Adaensemble: Learning adaptively sparse structured ensemble network for click-through rate prediction (2023). https://arxiv.org/abs/2301.08353
9. Yang, Y., Zhai, P.: Click-through rate prediction in online advertising: A literature review. Inform. Process. Manage. **59**(2), 102853 (Mar 2022). https://doi.org/10.1016/j.ipm.2021.102853
10. Zhen Ge, Wei Zhou, J.L., Ilardi, A.: Relevance constrained re-ranking in sponsored listing recommendations. In: Proceedings of AdKDD. ADKDD'14, Association for Computing Machinery, New York, NY, USA (2021)
11. Zhu, H., Jin, J., Tan, C., Pan, F., Zeng, Y., Li, H., Gai, K.: Optimized cost per click in taobao display advertising. CoRR **abs/1703.02091** (2017). http://arxiv.org/abs/1703.02091
12. Zhu, Y., Wang, G., Yang, J., Wang, D., Yan, J., Chen, Z.: Revenue optimization with relevance constraint in sponsored search, pp. 55–60. ADKDD '09, Association for Computing Machinery, New York, NY, USA (2009). https://doi.org/10.1145/1592748.1592756

More Ads, Happier Shoppers: Unified-Valuation Ad Allocation at Scale

Sergey Kolbin[1(✉)], Arushi Jain[3], Manavender Malgireddy[1], Kurt Zimmer[3], Masoum Mosmer[2], and Patrick Phelps[3]

[1] Wayfair LLC, Seattle, WA 98103, USA
{skolbin,mmalgireddy}@wayfair.com
[2] Wayfair LLC, Mountain View, CA 94041, USA
mmosmer@wayfair.com
[3] Wayfair LLC, Boston, MA 02116, USA
{jain31,kzimmer,pphelps}@wayfair.com

Abstract. Balancing short-term ad revenue with long-term user satisfaction is a central challenge in sponsored product search. We propose common currency, a unified ranking framework that merges sponsored and organic results within the same valuation. By translating predicted clicks and conversions into variable contribution dollars (VCD), both ad and organic items compete on a single, profit-based metric. We combine this objective with guardrails on relevance and ad load to preserve a high- quality customer experience. Our approach is implemented via a one-pass, order-preserving greedy merge, which we show is near-optimal in offline simulations despite the problem's inherent non-monotonicities. We also compare real-time and batch variants, finding that batch ranking recovers most of the profit uplift while incurring significantly less latency. In a six-week online experiment covering millions of keyword searches, our method allowed to expand ads footprint and increased ad revenue by 35% and, surprisingly, also improved conversion rates and long-term profit across ads and organic products together. These results suggest that when ads are relevant and well- spaced, elevating ad load can benefit both advertisers and end users, challenging the classic trade-off narrative. We discuss lessons learned from production deployment and outline directions for further enhancements.

Keywords: Sponsored Products Advertising · Ranking Optimization · Multi-objective Ranking · Profit Aware Optimization · Advertising Footprint · Profit-Relevance Tradeoff

1 Introduction

Sponsored product ads now shape the way millions of shoppers discover products online. Yet every additional ad competes with organic results for scarce real estate, forcing platforms to juggle three objectives that rarely align: (i) short-term ad revenue, (ii) short- and long-term retailer profit, and (iii) customer experience (e.g., measured by engagement and conversion rate CVR).

A. Bagherjeiran et al. (Eds.): AdKDD 2025, CCIS 2796, pp. 85–98, 2026.
https://doi.org/10.1007/978-3-032-16358-5_7

Status Quo and Blind Spots. A common approach on e-commerce search pages is a static footprint. This design (a) leaves material revenue untapped whenever relevant ads run out of slots, (b) ignores the profit margin of what shoppers actually buy, (c) cannot adapt to user ad tolerance. Recent feed-style work, notably Yan et al. [13], tackles a different setting: an endless-scroll newsfeed. They blend two pre-ranked lists (ads and organics) with a single shadow-price parameter and enforce simple guardrails—top-slot and min-gap between ads. However, their model optimizes expected ad revenue and engagement, not profit metrics like variable contribution dollars (VCD) that matter in retail. It also omits grid-specific UX rules such as max consecutive ads or organic-spacing quotas.

Our Approach. We formulate ad vs. organic allocation on product grids as a common currency optimization that prices every impression in dollar including ad revenue, variable contribution dollar (VCD - profit per sale), and a conversion guardrail:

$$u = \text{AdRevenue} + \text{pCVR}\big(\lambda + \text{VCD}\big),$$

subject to page-level relevance and fine-grained guardrails on density and spacing. Because those guardrails introduce only short-range dependencies, a single-pass *greedy merge* achieves >99% of the objective value of a more complex block-filling search.

Using two million historical searches we tuned the Lagrange multiplier λ and guardrails, then validated the policy in a six-week A/B test on U.S. traffic. Contrary to the classic "ad-fatigue" narrative, increasing the ads footprint simultaneously lifted ad revenue by 35%, and combined ads and organic VCD by 3% and CVR by 1%.

Our Key Contributions are:

1. **Unified-valuation ranking for e-commerce grids.** We extend the ads-vs-organic framework of Yan et al. [13] to product grids, incorporate profit (VCD) and viewability discounts, and add block-length and spacing guardrails tailored to product tiles.
2. **Linear-time greedy merge with near-optimality in practice.** A one-pass algorithm attains $\geq$99 % of the objective and is lightweight enough for production deployment.
3. **Large-scale evidence that more ads can be a *win–win*.** Offline simulations and a live A/B test show concurrent lifts in Ad Revenue, VCD, and CVR—demonstrating that higher ad density, when relevance-constrained, can enhance both monetization and shopper experience.
4. **Bridging science and production constraints.** We quantify the trade-off between real-time and weekly batch computation, showing that cached, keyword-level footprints recover most of the ad revenue upside with no additional serving latency.

2 Related Work

Balancing sponsored and organic content is a classical multiobjective optimization problem. Below we outline two research strands and position our "common-currency" footprinting work within that context.

Constrained and Multi-objective Optimization for Ad Insertion. Google's long-term experiments showed that short-run revenue lifts can erode lifetime value, motivating guard-rails on ad load and relevance [7]. A decade later, LinkedIn operationalized this idea at feed scale: a post-ranking merge maximizes revenue subject to an engagement constraint and simple UX rules [13]. JD.com generalized the approach by assigning virtual bids to organic items so that ads and organics compete in a single auction [4]. We follow the same line, but adapt it to an e-commerce grid: (i) we price conversions in variable contribution dollars (VCD), (ii) introduce max consecutive ads and organic spacing guardrails suited to product tiles, and (iii) bridge science complexity with production constraints (show that a greedy or batch approximations can deliver most of the value).

Re-examining the "Ad-Fatigue" Narrative. Google's long-horizon experiments famously showed that heavy ad loads can back-fire: extra sponsored links boosted short-run clicks yet reduced long-run usage once users learned to ignore clutter [7]. More recent evidence paints a subtler picture. Multi-objective ranking on Taobao raised both GMV and ad revenue in a 28-day test [14], and personalized ad-load policies on a 200-million-user social feed delivered simultaneous lifts in engagement and ad returns [11]. Optimized ad-pod scheduling on connected-TV streams likewise served additional ads while preserving viewer completion rates [8]. These studies suggest that when ads are relevant, well-spaced, and tailored to user tolerance, higher ad density need not erode organic engagement—in fact it can enhance overall value. Our own online experiment (Sect. 6) corroborates this emerging consensus: doubling ads footprint on grid search raised page-level CVR, VCD and long-term gross revenue and VCD, overturning the classic ad-fatigue concern in the context of Wayfair product search (Table 1).

3 Problem Formulation

3.1 Candidate Sets

Let $O = \{1, \ldots, |O|\}$ be the organic candidates and $A = \{1, \ldots, |A|\}$ the sponsored candidates. For each $j \in O$ we have the predicted conversion (per impression) rate pCVR^o_j and per-order profit VCD^o_j. For each $k \in A$ we know

$$\mathrm{ar}^a_k = \mathrm{pCTR}^a_k \cdot \mathrm{CPC}_k, \qquad \mathrm{pCVR}^a_k, \qquad \mathrm{VCD}^a_k,$$

where ar^a_k is the expected ad revenue in CPC model and is the product of predicted click-through rate pCTR^a_k and the clearing price CPC_k. Notice that our auction incorporates the floor price which bounds CPC_k from below.

Although the auction ranks ads by maximum bid, our page-level optimization uses the clearing price CPC_k instead. This aligns with Wayfair profit, removes the incentive to inflate bids, and follows the utility-vs-value perspective of [2,6].

Table 1. Notation used in Sect. 3

Symbol	Description
O, A	sets of organic and ad candidates
pCVR^o_j, pCVR^a_k	predicted conversion rate per impression
VCD^o_j, VCD^a_k	profit per order (short-term)
ar^a_k	expected ad revenue ($\mathrm{pCTR} \times \mathrm{CPC}$)
λ	shadow price of a conversion
δ_v	per-slot viewability discount
δ_s	per-slot offline slot-bias correction factor
C	minimum cumulative CVR
m	max consecutive ads
x	organic spacing multiplier after an ad block

3.2 Page Variables

We need to fill N product slots in search results. A binary vector $\mathbf{y} = (y_1, \ldots, y_N) \in \{0,1\}^N$ marks ads ($y_i = 1$) and organics ($y_i = 0$). Define

$$s(i,a) = \sum_{k=1}^{i} y_k, \quad s(i,o) = \sum_{k=1}^{i} (1 - y_k),$$

so $s(i,a)$ (resp. $s(i,o)$) is the running index of the ad (resp. organic) item placed in slot i.

3.3 Common-Currency Utility

We score each impression so that all terms can be expressed in currency (e.g. USD):

$$u^a_k = \mathrm{ar}^a_k + \mathrm{pCVR}^a_k(\lambda + \mathrm{VCD}^a_k), \qquad u^o_j = \mathrm{pCVR}^o_j(\lambda + \mathrm{VCD}^o_j).$$

The common currency formulas for ad and organic products are the same while recognizing that organic products do not generate ad revenue. The shadow value λ converts orders into the same units as profit and ad revenue (e.g. USD). With a slightly abuse of notation, we include λ directly into utility, see below for further details.

3.4 Objective

For each user search the objective is as follows:

$$\begin{aligned}\max_{y\in\{0,1\}^N} \quad & \sum_{i=1}^{N} \delta_v^i \cdot \left(y_i \cdot u^a_{s(i,a)} + (1-y_i)\cdot u^o_{s(i,o)}\right) \\ \text{s.t.} \quad & \sum_{i=1}^{N} \left[y_i \cdot \mathrm{pCVR}^a_{s(i,a)} + (1-y_i)\cdot \mathrm{pCVR}^o_{s(i,o)}\right] \geq C \quad \text{(Rel.)} \\ & \text{max ad block length } \leq m \quad \text{(LG-1)} \\ & \text{after ad block of length } b \text{ insert } \lfloor x\cdot b\rfloor \text{ organics} \quad \text{(LG-2)}\end{aligned} \tag{1}$$

$\delta_v \in (0,1]$ models viewability decay with scroll depth. Constraint (Rel.) enforces a minimum page CVR and allows us to determine the shadow value of an order λ (shared across all user searches) through offline simulations in Sect. 5. LG-1 caps any contiguous run of ads at m items ($m \leq 4$). LG-2 requires at least $\lfloor x \cdot b\rfloor$ organic results after an ad block of length b, rounded down for fractionals, with $x \in [0.5, 2]$.

Deduplication. If a product appears in both candidate sets, we keep its first occurrence and drop the duplicate; the same rule is applied in offline simulations.

Order-Preserving Fill vs. Footprint Stability. Our solver keeps the program-internal order produced by the Ads and Organic rankers as in [13]. This modularity means each team can evolve its model independently, but it also ties total footprint to upstream rank changes (e.g., if one program wants to boost certain products, its average pCVR declines reducing footprint). We tested an order-agnostic version that first re-ranks all product candidates based on common currency and only then decides the footprint; it hurt key metrics in offline simulations due to the wedge in footprint determination and actual SKUs placed. We therefore accept the order-preserving trade-off and plan to manage long-term stability by tuning λ, tightening guardrails, or rolling out boosting changes symmetrically across programs.

4 Merge Algorithms

Below we present two constructive heuristics that build a merged page slot by slot from the pre-ranked Ad and Organic lists. Even though we decided to proceed with Greedy in practice, we evaluated that the loss is small relative to a more optimal approximate solution.

4.1 Greedy Merge (Algorithm 1)

Algorithm 1 is a single-pass $O(N)$ merge identical in structure to the rule used by [13]. Function `GuardrailsOK`(L,m,x) returns true if appending one more ad to the currently merged list L keeps the current contiguous ad block $\leq m$ and we already placed at least $\lfloor x\cdot b\rfloor$ organics after the last ad block.

Algorithm 1: GREEDY MERGE

Input: ranked organics $L^o[1 \dots |O|]$, ranked ads $L^a[1 \dots |A|]$; max ad-block length m, spacing factor x; target page length N

Output: merged list $L[1 \dots N]$

$j_o \leftarrow 1,\ j_a \leftarrow 1$
while $j_o + j_a \le N$ **do**
  if $j_a \le |A|$ ***and*** $u^a_{j_a} > u^o_{j_o}$ ***and*** `GuardrailsOK`(L, m, x) **then**
    L.append$(L^a_{j_a})$;
    $j_a{+}{+}$
  else
    L.append$(L^o_{j_o})$;
    $j_o{+}{+}$
  end
end
return L

4.2 Block-Filling Search (Algorithm 2)

Why Greedy is Sub-optimal. Each program's list is internally monotone in its own score, yet the common-currency utilities $\{u^a, u^o\}$ need not be monotone. Consider filling $N = 3$ slots with common currency utilities for ads as $(0.02, 0.06, 0.03)$ and organic as $(0.04, 0.03, 0.02)$. Greedy places the 0.04 Organic first for the total of $0.04 + 0.03 + 0.02 = 0.09$. The optimal layout starts with two Ads and achieves $0.02 + 0.06 + 0.04 = 0.12$. Greedy's myopic, slot-by-slot choice cannot foresee that a slightly worse item now may unlock a much better one next.

BLOCKFILL Approach. We propose a more optimal approach that would result in an optimal solution for the example above. The approach considers all possible combinations of ad block lengths for each decision whether to put an ad and thus also has a linear complexity of $O(Nm)$ (with $m \le 4$ in practice).

Empirical Comparison. We compared two approaches in offline simulations (not reported for brevity) and observed that GREEDY MERGE consistently achieves $\ge 99\%$ of BLOCKFILL objective across guardrail and constraint combinations. The negligible gain does not justify the added complexity, so we proceeded with GREEDY MERGE for further simulations and tests. We leave finding the exact solution for future work.

5 Offline Simulation Study

Offline simulations let us stress-test candidate footprint policies, select the Lagrange multiplier λ, and pick customer-experience guardrails without touching live traffic.

Algorithm 2: BLOCKFILL (m-slot look-ahead)

Input: same inputs as Algorithm 1
Output: merged list $L[1 \ldots N]$

$j_o \leftarrow 1,\ j_a \leftarrow 1$
while $j_o + j_a \leq N$ **do**
  for $b \leftarrow 0$ **to** m **do**
    $U_b \leftarrow \sum_{t=0}^{b-1} \delta_v^t u_{j_a+t}^a + \sum_{t=0}^{m-b-1} \delta_v^{b+t} u_{j_o+t}^o$
    discard U_b if the block $(b, m-b)$ violates guardrails
  end
  $b^\star \leftarrow \arg\max_b U_b$
  if $b^\star > 0$ *(can put ads preserving guardrails)* **then**
    $L.\text{append}\big(L^a[j_a : j_a + b^\star - 1]\big)$
    $j_a \leftarrow j_a + b^\star$
  else
    $L.\text{append}(L^o_{j_o})$
    j_o++
  end
end
return L

5.1 Data and Pre-processing

Raw Data. We use a sample of 4M user keyword searches on Wayfair U.S. traffic for the two weeks before the A/B launch. We split these searches into the training set (first week) to generate the footprints and evaluation set (second week). Each user search (e.g., "red sofa") yields several hundred ad *and* organic candidates per query, each with:

- predicted conversion rate pCVR, same deep learning model applied to both ads and organic products
- variable contribution dollars VCD,
- for ads only: predicted click-through rate pCTR and cost-per-click CPC outcome from the advertising auction.

Keyword Coverage. We retain and report the results for the evaluation set based only on the keywords that are present in the training set - this helps us approximate how the cached (batch) footprint would perform in production. Replaying a cache that is one week old introduces negligible staleness in practice. For the long tail of new user searches that are not covered by keyword based batches, we developed an approach relying on a higher level aggregation (e.g., product class instead of keyword) and that was not included in the original test, see Conclusion for further details.

Position-Bias Correction. Because the models are position-agnostic, we down-weight engagement predictions by a slot-specific factor, e.g., pCVR $\leftarrow$ pCVR $\cdot \delta_s^i$ with $\delta_s \in (0,1)$. Without this adjustment, bottom-of-page pCTR and pCVR would be overstated more than $2\times$, distorting the offline projections. Notice that δ_s^i is the correction for model bias and would not be needed had the models contained slot as a feature, while δ_v^i is an independent discount that captures user behavior.

5.2 Metrics

For both offline simulations and online tests we track two complementary metric groups that are expected to capture both advertising program growth and overall company goals including user experience. We do not simulate ROAS and gross revenue, but report those outcomes in the online test.

Advertising Key Metrics

- **Ad revenue**: $\widehat{\text{Rev}} = \sum_i \delta_v^i \cdot \text{pCTR}_i \cdot \text{CPC}_i$
- **Ad clicks**: $\widehat{\text{Clicks}} = \sum_i \delta_v^i \cdot \text{pCTR}_i$
- **Footprint**: number of ad slots on a page $= \sum_i y_i$ (distinct from impressions because many users do not scroll)

Advertising + Organic Joint Metrics

- **CVR**: $\widehat{\text{CVR}} = \frac{1}{N} \sum_i \delta_v^i \cdot \text{pCVR}_i$
- **VCD**: $\widehat{\text{VCD}} = \sum_i \delta_v^i \cdot \text{pCVR}_i \cdot \text{VCD}_i$

5.3 Selecting the Policy to Test

Guardrail Search. For each combination of *max ad–block length* $m \in \{2,4\}$ and *spacing multiplier* $x \in \{1.5, 2.0\}$ we sweep the Lagrange multiplier λ and record the resulting *Ad-Revenue*–vs–*CVR* frontier. Figure 1 shows four such frontiers: the looser guardrails ($m = 4, x = 1.5$) dominate the stricter ($m = 2, x = 2$) alternative across the entire curve, so we adopt the orange policy for the A/B test (orange star) with specific λ value chosen based on the business trade-off between CVR and ad revenue. Notice this value of λ is also high enough to be consistent with the long-term impact of a generated conversion on company's long-term VCD (purchases today stimulate purchases in the future).

Production Baseline. The black star marks the live static-footprint policy (ads fixed in slots 2, 4, 8, 9, 14, 15). Extending that static list would shift the dashed line up (revenue) and left (lower CVR), but the incremental gains are far smaller than those available from dynamic footprints, so we did not pursue larger static layouts.

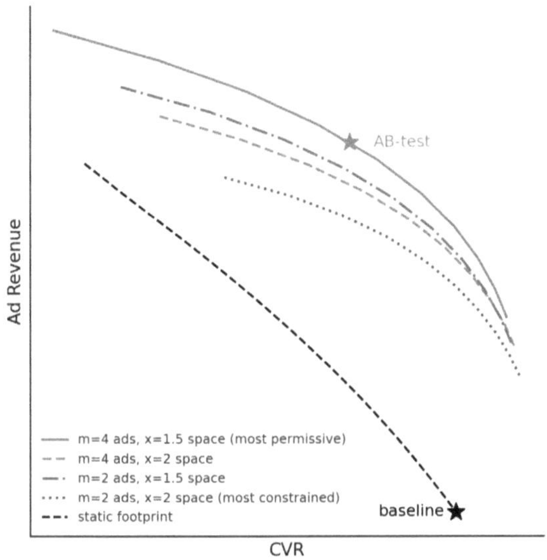

Fig. 1. Guardrail trade-off. Each colored curve is the *Ad-Revenue–CVR* frontier for a guardrail pair (m, x); the dashed line is the static baseline. Stars mark the production policy (black) and the A/B allocation (orange). Units suppressed for commercial sensitivity.

5.4 Offline Simulation: Results and Trade-Offs

In the previous section we used simulations to confirm that we are more likely to succeed with a dynamic footprint approach and selected a specific set of guardrails. We now perform additional simulations to achieve two additional goals: 1) decide whether we want to build a real time system vs. using a batch approach and 2) determine if we want to test a version without VCD.

Table 2. Offline-simulation lifts vs. a static-footprint baseline (positive = better). RT = real-time ranker, Batch = daily batch ranker, NoVCD = value function without the VCD term.

	RT–VCD	RT–NoVCD	Batch–VCD	Batch–NoVCD
Panel A: Advertising Metrics				
Ad revenue	38.7	48.1	38.1	46.9
Ad clicks	39.9	46.0	39.4	45.5
Avg. footprint lift	99.3	104.3	103.6	108.3
Panel B: Advertising + Organic Metrics				
CVR	0.3	0.5	−0.8	−0.8
VCD	3.0	−0.6	0.7	−1.0

Real-Time (RT) vs. Batch - Motivation. Algorithms described in Sect. 4 determine optimal footprints given data inputs per each user search. If we want to apply those algorithms as is in production, we then would need a real time implementation as we will have to rely on scoring model outputs such as pCTR and pCVR. Unfortunately, real time solutions are usually more complex to implement in practice as that would require more synchronization between the ads and organic systems to combine both ads and organic score inputs inside the footprint system. Real-time solutions can also increase latency due to both synchronization and the need to fetch additional inputs such as bids or VCD. Therefore we consider an alternative, a batch solution in which we precompute footprints for each keyword, taking the footprint of the median length over all user searches for that keyword in the past week. Notice that we can compare the two approaches in offline simulations as the required inputs are logged in our system per each user search.

Real-Time (RT) vs. Batch - Outcome. Table 2 reports the outcome of our simulation analysis and shows that RT can generate more ad revenue (+0.6–1.2%), higher CVR (+1.1–1.3%) and VCD (+1.6–2.3%) while requiring lower ad footprint. While these differences are important, we decided to implement the first online test using the Batch approach due to faster time to production and still noticeable ad revenue opportunity.

Effect of the VCD Term. When we include the VCD component (RT-VCD and Batch-VCD), we observe higher projected VCD (+1.7–3.6%) but lower ad revenue (-8.8%-9.4%), so we test both the VCD and no-VCD settings in production. We include the no-VCD version because of higher ad revenue and we generally expect that ad revenue simulation predictions would be more accurate (e.g., ad revenue is based on clicks that are easier to predict due to more click data).

Ad Revenue vs. Footprint. Projected ad revenue increases are smaller than footprint increases - while we can allow ads to take over more slots, those slots are often at the bottom of the page and so are viewed and clicked less often by the users.

Reproducibility. All simulations run in Google BigQuery with the ranking logic expressed as embedded JavaScript UDFs, enabling end-to-end offline simulation reruns from a single SQL script.

6 Online Experiments

We ran a six-week A/B test on Wayfair's U.S. keyword search traffic, comparing two batch-computed policies (Batch–VCD and Batch–NoVCD) with the production static footprint (all variants received 1/3 of traffic randomized by user id hash). All reported lifts are percentage changes versus baseline.

Additional Metric Details. In the online A/B results we also report ROAS (Return on Ad Spend) and gross revenue - these guardrail metrics were not included in the offline simulations. While we report impression-level CVR, VCD, and gross revenue metrics in Panel B, we also confirmed that the results are consistent on page or user session levels. The online gains mirror the direction of our offline projections but are modestly smaller, as simulation estimates do not fully capture serving-time noise and model error. To tighten this offline–online gap, we are evaluating counterfactual-estimation approaches such as Nguyen et al. [9] for the future (Table 3).

Table 3. Online A/B percentage lifts; bold values are significant at $p < 0.05$ (two-sided t-test).

	Batch–VCD	Batch–NoVCD
Panel A: Advertising Metrics		
Ad revenue	**28.3**	**35.0**
Ad clicks	**28.3**	**31.7**
Avg. footprint lift	**78.3**	**81.7**
ROAS	**7.4**	**5.9**
Panel B: Advertising + Organic Metrics		
CVR	−0.7	**1.0**
VCD	1.2	**2.7**
Gross revenue	0.4	**2.6**
Panel C: Long-Term Site-Wide Projections		
VCD	0.3	**0.6**
Gross revenue	0.3	**0.6**

Win–Win Lift. Both treatments increased ad revenue, and the Batch–NoVCD arm additionally produced statistically significant lifts in page-level CVR, VCD, gross revenue, and ROAS. Prior work shows that heavy or poorly targeted ad loads can depress engagement and retention [3,5]. Here we moved from six ads per page to a still-conservative footprint of average 12 out of 48 slots per page chosen based on expected common-currency utility under pCVR guardrails. For some keywords we showed fewer ads than before (e.g. when ads had much lower pCVR than organic products). The extra ads were often more relevant than the displaced organic results, consistent with advertisers exploiting keyword-level gaps to surface high-intent products that organic ranking misses. Our findings align with recent evidence that carefully allocated, high-relevance ads can benefit both users and platforms [11], demonstrating that ad load need not be a zero-sum trade-off when relevance constraints are enforced.

Batch--NoVCD Outperforms the VCD-Aware Variant. The simpler Batch–NoVCD arm delivered significantly higher ad clicks, ad revenue, and page-level CVR/gross revenue, and even showed a (non-significant) lift in VCD—paradoxically surpassing the variant that optimizes VCD directly. This underscores a pragmatic lesson: enriching an objective with extra terms does not guarantee better business outcomes. A likely culprit is estimation noise: predicting VCD is harder than predicting clicks or conversions, so errors propagate into the footprint and erode gains. Offline–online gaps of this sort are well documented in large-scale ad systems [10]. Closing them will require higher-fidelity VCD models or uncertainty-aware objectives, which we leave for future work.

Long-Term Durability. Ad-fatigue can reverse early gains [7], so we ran both variants through Wayfair's Long-Term Impact Estimation Platform, which extrapolates effects via the surrogate-index method of Athey et al. [1]. Using 42 days of experiment data, the platform projects metrics out to 168 days across the entire site (i.e., beyond keyword search covered by our experiment). The forecasts show positive lifts in both VCD and gross revenue; only the Batch–NoVCD arm is statistically significant, but the direction is consistent for both. Hence the short-run revenue uplift is unlikely to be clawed back by latent ad-fatigue and is expected to translate into durable profit.

7 Conclusion and Future Work

Conclusion. We deployed a unified–valuation "common currency" ranker that prices ads and organics in the same profit-based units, then merges the two lists via a one-pass greedy algorithm. We evaluated both real time and batch version and demonstrated the relative efficiency of a simpler batch approach in offline simulations, providing a path to apply our approach under a variety of ad and organic system designs (e.g., whether or not it's easy to connect ads and organic score inputs in real time). In production, the system allowed scaling footprint expansion and raised ad revenue by 35 % while also lifting page-level CVR and long-term profit, providing another example that carefully chosen ads can break a common revenue–UX trade-off.

Future Work. Next steps fall into four tracks. (1) Broader reuse: our batch framework already supports footprints for unseen keywords by applying footprints fitted for predicted class of the user search and can further be applied in other context such as carousels in product pages based on anchor product. (2) Real time ranking: offline experiments suggest additional CVR and VCD gains from recomputing footprints on the fly; implementing this low-latency pipeline is our main engineering goal. (3) Stronger profit signals: we can try refining our VCD modeling so that profitability can become a direct optimization objective. (4) Developing more personalized ad supply focusing on user preferences for ads (e.g., such as in [12]).

References

1. Athey, S., Chetty, R., Imbens, G.W., Kang, H.: The surrogate index: combining short-term proxies to estimate long-term treatment effects more rapidly and precisely. NBER Working Paper 26463, National Bureau of Economic Research (2019). http://www.nber.org/papers/w26463. Accessed Aug 2024
2. Balseiro, S.R., et al.: A field guide for pacing budget and ROS constraints. In: Proceedings of the 41st International Conference on Machine Learning (ICML 2024). Proceedings of Machine Learning Research, vol. 235, pp. 2607–2638. PMLR, Vienna, Austria (2024). https://proceedings.mlr.press/v235/balseiro24a.html, arXiv:2302.08530
3. Broder, A.Z., et al.: To swing or not to swing: learning when (not) to advertise. In: Proceedings of the 17th ACM International Conference on Information and Knowledge Management (CIKM 2008), pp. 1003–1012 (2008)
4. Carrion, C., et al.: Blending advertising with organic content in e-commerce: a virtual bids optimization approach. In: Proceedings of the 37th AAAI Conference on Artificial Intelligence (AAAI 2023), pp. 15476–15484. AAAI Press, Washington, DC (2023). https://doi.org/10.1609/aaai.v37i13.26835
5. Goli, A., Reiley, D.H., Zhang, H.: Personalizing ad load to optimize subscription and ad revenues: product strategies constructed from experiments on pandora. Mark. Sci. **44**(2), 327–352 (2025). https://doi.org/10.1287/mksc.2022.0357
6. Golrezaei, N., Lobel, I., Leme, R.P.: Auction design for ROI-constrained buyers. In: Proceedings of the Web Conference 2021 (WWW 2021), pp. 1007–1018. ACM, Ljubljana, Slovenia (2021). https://doi.org/10.1145/3442381.3449841
7. Hohnhold, H., O'Brien, D., Tang, D.: Focusing on the long-term: it's good for users and business. In: Proceedings of the 21st ACM SIGKDD International Conference on Knowledge Discovery and Data Mining (KDD 2015), pp. 1849–1858. ACM, Sydney, Australia (2015). https://doi.org/10.1145/2783258.2788583
8. Kumawat, N., Vajpai, M., Varshney, N.: Programmatic optimization of ad pods for maximizing consumer engagement and revenue. In: Proceedings of the 16th ACM AdKDD Workshop on Advertising and E–Commerce (AdKDD 2022), Washington, DC, USA (2022). https://adkdd.org/2022/papers/adkdd22-kumawat-programmatic.pdf
9. Nguyen, P.H., Gligorijevic, D., Borah, A., Adalinge, G., Bagherjeiran, A.: Practical budget pacing algorithms and a simulation test-bed for eBay marketplace sponsored search. In: Proceedings of the 2023 ACM AdKDD Workshop on Advertising and E–Commerce. ACM, Long Beach, CA, USA (2023)
10. Qian, C., et al.: Handling online–offline discrepancy in pinterest ads ranking system (2024). https://medium.com/pinterest-engineering/handling-online-offline-discrepancy-in-pinterest-ads-ranking-system-8fd662da4c2d. pinterest Engineering Blog. Accessed 18 May 2025
11. Sagtani, H., Jhawar, M.G., Mehrotra, R., Jeunen, O.: Ad-load balancing via off-policy learning in a content marketplace. In: Proceedings of the 17th ACM International Conference on Web Search and Data Mining (WSDM 2024), pp. 586–595. ACM, Mérida, México (2024). https://doi.org/10.1145/3616855.3635846
12. Shi, W., et al.: Ads supply personalization via doubly robust learning. In: Proceedings of the 33rd ACM International Conference on Information and Knowledge Management (CIKM 2024), pp. 4874–4881. Association for Computing Machinery, New York, NY, USA (2024). https://doi.org/10.1145/3627673.3680035

13. Yan, J., Xu, Z., Tiwana, B., Chatterjee, S.: Ads allocation in feed via constrained optimization. In: Proceedings of the 26th ACM SIGKDD Conference on Knowledge Discovery and Data Mining (KDD 2020), pp. 3386–3394. ACM, Virtual Event (2020). https://doi.org/10.1145/3394486.3403391
14. Zheng, Y., et al.: Multi-objective personalized product retrieval in taobao search. arXiv preprint arXiv:2210.04170 (2022). https://doi.org/10.48550/arXiv.2210.04170

DCN²: Interplay of *Implicit* Collision Weights and *Explicit* Cross Layers for Large-Scale Recommendation

Blaž Škrlj(✉), Yonatan Karni, Grega Gašperšič, Blaž Mramor, Yulia Stolin, Martin Jakomin, Jasna Urbančič, Yuval Dishi, Natalia Silberstein, Ophir Friedler, and Assaf Klein

Teads, New York, USA
{blaz.skrlj,yonatan.karni,grega.gaspersic,blaz.mramor, yulia.stolin,martin.jakomin,jasna.urbancic,yuval.dishi, natalia.silberstein,ophir.friedler,assaf.klein}@teads.com

Abstract. The Deep and Cross architecture (DCNv2) is a robust production baseline and is integral to numerous real-life recommender systems. Its inherent efficiency and ability to model interactions often result in models that are both simpler and highly competitive compared to more computationally demanding alternatives, such as Deep FFMs. In this work, we introduce three significant algorithmic improvements to the DCNv2 architecture, detailing their formulation and behavior at scale. The enhanced architecture we refer to as DCN^2 is actively used in a live recommender system, processing over 0.5 billion predictions per second across diverse use cases where it out-performed DCNv2, both offline and online (a/b tests). These improvements effectively address key limitations observed in the DCNv2, including information loss in Cross layers, implicit management of collisions through learnable lookup-level weights, and explicit modeling of pairwise similarities with a custom layer that emulates FFMs' behavior. The superior performance of DCN^2 is also demonstrated on four publicly available benchmark data sets.

Keywords: Recommender systems · Deep&Cross · Algorithms

1 Introduction

Contemporary *recommender systems* are composed of various components, with **factorization-machine-based models** playing a critical role in large-scale applications. These machine learning models are favored for their ability to deliver fast inference while maintaining strong predictive performance. While the original *factorization machines* (FMs) [10] served as a generalization of logistic regression, advancements have led to more sophisticated architectures, such as Deep and Cross Networks (DCN) [14]. The second iteration, DCNv2 [15], successfully addressed scalability and performance issues, maintaining its status as a leading neural network architecture for tasks like click-through rate

A. Bagherjeiran et al. (Eds.): AdKDD 2025, CCIS 2796, pp. 99–112, 2026.
https://doi.org/10.1007/978-3-032-16358-5_8

and conversion prediction. Despite DCNv2's capabilities, certain algorithmic aspects remain sub-optimal. It lacks a specific mechanism for *collision* management, i.e. accounting for effects of multiple items having same representation [4], often deferring this responsibility to external hashing logic. Moreover, although **Cross layers** are theoretically advantageous for modeling higher-order interactions, they may suffer from information loss due to the compression inherent to each intermediary projection. Additionally, the algorithmic bias in Cross networks differs from that of Field-aware Factorization Machines (FFMs), where performance trade-offs have been extensively optimized (explicit interactions). Contributions of this paper are multifold: We present DCN^2, an architecture building on DCNv2, designed to address issues related to collision handling, algorithmic bias in pairwise interactions, and lossiness of Cross layers; the **collision handling mechanism** ensures lookup-level weights can modulate impact of new collisions, pairwise interactions are explicitly handled as we show that DCNv2 does not entail all, and the cross layer itself was improved to capture more fine-grained interaction patterns and lose less information layer-to-layer. The performance of DCN^2 is evaluated against DCNv2 using four real-life benchmark datasets, demonstrating competitive results, as well as within a live recommender that handles more than 0.5 billion pps, where the new architecture significantly out-performs the existing DCNv2 based model (+3% RPM). We outline the deployment pathway for DCN^2, which now serves as the flagship

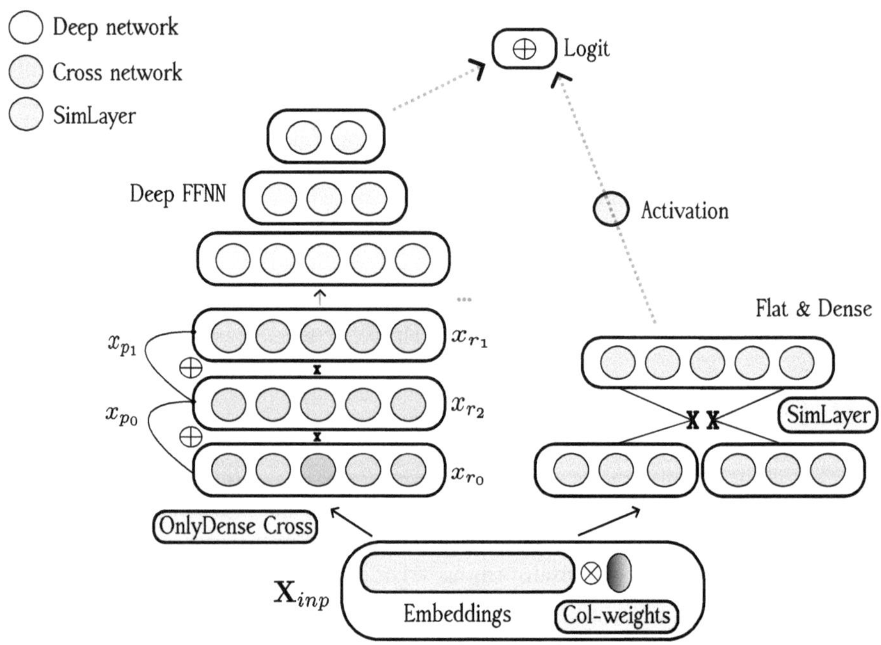

Fig. 1. Architecture of DCN^2. Parts marked in green denote additions on top of DCNv2 [15] presented in this paper. (Color figure online)

model, processing over 0.5 billion predictions per second across diverse applications. Insights and battle scars from optimizing online performance in a live recommender are discussed, including inference optimization, model migration, and handling of multi-value features.

2 Related Work

Web-scale recommender systems have in recent years converged to a combination of predictive models, combined with filtering/sorting tailored to a given use case [3]. **Factorization machine** based approaches became the gold standard methodology for estimating click-through rates, conversions or similar. This branch of methods extends the commonly used logistic regression based classifiers by incorporating either explicit or implicit notion of feature interaction. One significant extension to the paradigm of myopic LR are factorization machines (FM) [10]. This branch of approaches attempts to explicitly or implicitly model interactions between features (or directly their values). Recent extensions of this paradigm include higher-order factorization machines [2], field-aware factorization machines [6] and Deep FFMs [12]. Further, with the advent of GPU-based compute, deep learning-based approaches started to dominate in this domain. Approaches such as AutoInt [13] exploit the attention layer-like mechanism to automatically unveil relevant interactions. Recent approaches also investigated use of Graph Neural Network-like patterns for building factorization machines [16]. Computational efficiency, however, remains one of the key aspects of factorization machine based approaches in real-life production. One of the methods that moved the boundary between both compute efficiency and predictive performance are the Deep&Cross networks (DCNv2 [15]). This type of neural network architecture introducess the *Cross* layers, a mechanism that models higher order interactions via iterative building of the latent space between the initial embeddings (inputs). The DCNv2 architecture remains one of the top-performing, off-the-shelf solutions for building larger-scale recommender systems. Insights obtained as part of research related to DCNv2 have been integrated into widely used deep learning frameworks such as Tensorflow [1]. Simultaneously to research on neural network architectures, inspection of the impact of *collisions*, i.e. same-representation multi-item occurrences, became a lively research area of its own. Approaches that mitigate negative impacts of collisions are discussed next. One prominent direction is by incorporating *semantic IDs*, high-level identifiers that preserve semantic meaning of items [19]. Alternatively, approaches that parametrize the hash space to mitigate collision impact (i.e. learning-to-collide) have also shown promising results [5]. Real-life systems such as Monolith [8] implement the collisionless principle – re-hashing of items if required to preserve collision-free embedding space. Mitigating the **issue of collisions** is paramount when designing a modern recommender system, as otherwise loss of predictive performance is expected regardless of architecture details [7]. This work sources from both areas of research and proposes an architecture that operates at the level of DCNv2, yet is better suited for high-velocity real-life data streams where negative impact of collisions becomes prominent in time.

3 DCN^2 Architecture

This section focuses on DCN^2 architecture, key components, relation to DCNv2 and its computational complexity. Schematic overview of the architecture with main highlighted differences to DCNv2 is shown in Fig. 1.

3.1 Collision-Weighted Lookups

The first algorithmic improvement stems from the observation that, regardless of the lookup table size, collision rates are high for realistic data streams. Instead of resorting to dedicated hashing schemes as many existing approaches, we propose an alternative that is more intrinsic to the neural network itself. Instead of explicitly attempting to reduce collisions, we introduce a weight for each lookup. The weight is initially set to 1.0, implying it has no impact on the existing lookup scheme. However, in time, weights per lookups change with regards to either new items, or collision-induced effects. By being able to quickly modify importance of each lookup, we noticed the neural network is able to adapt to new parts of the stream faster, yielding significant performance improvement in terms of relative information gain (RIG) [17]. For example, changes of publishers in the data stream (appearing/disappearing) require new embeddings, implying they will be shared at representation level eventually. The collision weights are formulated as follows[1]. Let $\mathbf{X}_e \in \mathbb{R}^{b \times d}$ represent the commonly considered item embedding table; b is the set of possible lookups (table's capacity) and d the embedding dimension. Next, consider a table with one additional dimension ($\mathbf{X} \in \mathbb{R}^{b \times (d+1)}$) that has the following initialization structure:

$$\mathbf{X}_{ec} = \begin{cases} \mathbf{X}[:, 1:d] = \mathbf{X}[:, 1:d]; -\omega \leq \mathcal{N}(\mu, \sigma^2) \leq \omega, \\ \mathbf{X}[:, d+1] = \mathbb{1} \end{cases}$$

where $\mathbf{X}_{ec}$ represents the new embedding matrix, and $\mathcal{N}$ the standard normal distribution. ω denotes allowed bound for the values. Having defined the partitioned matrix, we further define the main lookup operation as follows.

$$\mathbf{X}_{\text{inp}} = \mathbf{X}_{ec}[:, \ldots d] \odot \mathbf{X}_{ec}[:, d+1],$$

where $\odot$ denotes row-scalar products between the embedding matrix and the weight vector ($\mathbb{1}$). By definition, the initial structure can be interpreted as a generalization of the embedding matrix where all collision weights are equal to one, thus no impact of the collision weights is expected. However, these weights are differentiable, and are subject to updates alongside the main embedding space (they change in time, reducing the importance of frequently colliding items). The

[1] This idea was inspired by notion of polysemanticity in LLMs [11].

additional computational overhead is bounded by $\mathcal{O}(|X|)$ additional multiplications per lookup (scalar-matrix multiplication), and is in practice not significant (relative to the remainder of the architecture, these multiplications represent the minority of compute time).

3.2 *onlydense* Layer as an Alternative to Cross

The Cross layer that we use is a slight modification of the basic Cross layer from Sect. 3.2, [15]. Although the actual implementation of the DCN v2 Cross layer, see Sect. 3.5 in [15], offers more efficient neural networks via it's low-rank mixture architecture, it exhibits information loss due to the projective nature of subsequent applications of the layer – each Cross application first projects the input to a lower dimension, where it performs the cross operation[2]. We noticed that we can achieve similar, or better predictive performance with fewer Cross layers, which perform explicit feature crosses. We refer to this iteration of the Cross layer as the *onlydense* layer[3], as it intuitively performs all crosses in the intrinsic dense space (not projected). The low-rank Cross layer's formulation is as follows [15],

$$\begin{aligned} x_p &= \alpha(\mathbf{W}_0 \cdot \mathbf{x} + b_0) \\ x_o &= \mathbf{W}_1 \cdot x_p + b_1 + \phi \cdot \mathbf{x} \\ x_r &= x_0 \odot x_o + \mathbf{x}, \end{aligned}$$

where $W_0 \in \mathbb{R}^{d\times p}, W_1 \in \mathbb{R}^{p\times d}$ and d and p denote the output and the projection dimensions, respectively. In contrast, the *onlydense* counter-part presented in this work is defined as

$$\begin{aligned} x_t &= \alpha(\mathbf{W} \cdot \mathbf{x} + b_0) \\ x_r &= x_t \odot \mathbf{x} \cdot \phi. \end{aligned}$$

Here, α denotes the activation function (ReLU in practice) and $\mathbf{W} \in \mathbb{R}^{d\times d}$. The equation represents an *explicit* cross projection operation, followed by an anchor mapping achieved via a scaled Hadamard product[4]. Note that the proposed layer does not perform element-wise summation, but performs only multiplication of the inputs with activated weight space of the same dimension, further scaled via a factor. Note also the absence of x_o - the anchor multiplication considered by DCNv2 Cross layer – DCN^2 operates not by anchoring each Cross operation with initial embedding values x_0, but rather iterative multiplication in the same dimension[5] (Fig. 2).

[2] Formal argument for proving exact information loss bounds via Rank-Nullity Theorem is beyond the scope of this paper.

[3] Name stems from the observation that dense layers with input coupling yield sufficient performance.

[4] In practice ϕ has values between 1.0 and 3.0.

[5] Note that for the case of a single layer, we can assume $x = x_0$.

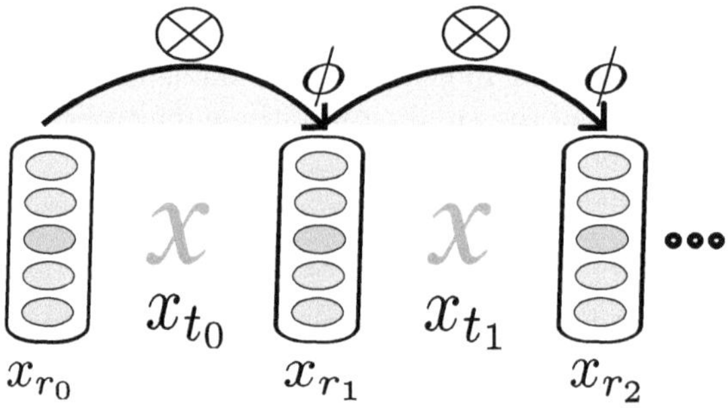

Fig. 2. Example with two hidden *onlydense* layers.

In terms of computational complexity, the *onlydense* layer is $O(d^2)$, same as the basic Cross layer from [15], and thus obviously heavier than the low-rank Cross layer, which is $O(d \cdot p)$. However, we observed a trade-off between computational complexity and the expressiveness of *onlydense*: The latter, as shown in offline and online experiments in the remainder of this paper, offers practical benefits, making DCN^2 a suitable candidate for large-scale production[6].

Table 1. Performance of DCN^2 on benchmark data sets (AUC aggregates, window of 20k). Highlighted rows show top-performing approach w.r.t. average AUC. Highlighted are top-performing algorithms (or the ones with lowest values in case of min/std).

Avazu						Criteo					
Algorithm	avg	median	max	min	std	Algorithm	avg	median	max	min	std
FM	0.7748	0.7746	0.8304	0.7237	0.0180	FM	0.7834	0.7831	0.8166	0.7617	0.0064
deepFM	0.7812	0.7814	0.8350	0.7230	0.0183	deepFM	0.7906	0.7904	0.8214	0.7716	0.0063
DCNv2	0.7826	0.7832	0.8351	0.7244	0.0183	DCNv2	0.7922	0.7918	0.8229	0.7730	0.0063
DCN^2	0.7846	0.7846	0.8387	0.7284	0.0183	**DCN^2**	0.7933	0.7930	0.8231	0.7751	0.0063
DCN^2-simk	0.7824	0.7826	0.8354	0.7242	0.0183	**DCN^2**-simk	0.7922	0.7919	0.8233	0.7738	0.0063
KDD2012						iPinYou					
Algorithm	avg	median	max	min	std	Algorithm	avg	median	max	min	std
FM	0.7547	0.7545	0.8336	0.6769	0.0201	FM	0.7521	0.7572	0.9955	0.3638	0.1049
deepFM	0.7719	0.7677	0.8709	0.7058	0.0260	deepFM	0.7669	0.7683	0.9961	0.4275	0.0997
DCNv2	0.7730	0.7684	0.8731	0.7133	0.0265	DCNv2	0.7659	0.7667	0.9975	0.4333	0.1001
DCN^2	0.7747	0.7699	0.8735	0.7051	0.0272	**DCN^2**	0.7561	0.7615	0.9984	0.3574	0.1023
DCN^2-simk	0.7733	0.7693	0.8761	0.7105	0.0266	**DCN^2**-simk	0.7467	0.7518	0.9980	0.4181	0.1043

[6] The inequality that governs the trade-off is $l_{od} \cdot (|F| \cdot d) \leq l_c \cdot ((|F| \cdot d)/d_{\text{Cross}})$; F denotes feature set l_{od} *onlydense* layer count, and d dimension (left-hand side is the *onlydense* layer.

3.3 Making Pairwise Interactions Explicit

Field-aware Factorization Machines (FFMSs) are amongst the most expressive types of architectures (especially their deep counter-parts). However, integrating them directly alongside Deep/Cross layers incurs a substantial computational overhead, and is in practice infeasible. To remedy this shortcoming, we propose a substantially simplifed version of the FFM idea, inspired by [9], vectorized in the form of a single dot product + projection at the pairwise interaction level (SimLayer in Fig. 1). We observed that including this layer complements the Deep/Cross part, indicating that the algorithmic bias of this layer is complementary to that of DCNv2. The layer can be formulated as

$$\hat{y}_{\text{sk}} = \alpha\left(\sum_{i=1}^{n}\sum_{j=1}^{n} \mathbf{w}_{k'(i,j)}\left(\sum_{k=1}^{m} \mathbf{e}_{ik}\cdot\mathbf{e}_{jk}\right) + b\right),$$

where $\mathbf{e}_{ij}$ corresponds to an indexed input embedding, and $\mathbf{w}_{k'(i,j)}$ to the mapping from matrix indices to the flattened vector index (m and n denote representation dimensions). The output activation is denoted by α. The layer directly models pairwise interactions between embeddings via (activated) dot-product based similarity calculation. Albeit *redundant* (there are two representations per interaction), we noticed directly multiplying the matrices is faster than doing slicing/sub-setting on the fly. Over-parametrizing each interaction also showed no loss in predictive performance w.r.t. single-parameter implementation. The layer is conceptually aligned with the FFM idea in the sense that it explicitly computes feature pairs via factorization, even though it diverges when considering the activation part. Finally, we noticed that the best way to integrate this layer with the existing DCN stack is to include it as an additional *logit* – directly into the final layer of the neural network as $\hat{y}_f = \sigma(\hat{y}_{dcn} + \hat{y}_{sk} + b_f)$, here, $\hat{y}_f$ denotes the final prediction, $\hat{y}_{dcn}$ the output of the DCN part of the architecture and $\hat{y}_{sk}$ the output of the similarity layer. The b_f represents the bias term and σ the sigmoid activation.

4 Benchmarks on Open Data Sets

We proceed by presenting the performance on known data sets. The experimental setting was conducted as follows. We considered the following data sets; Criteo[7], Avazu[8], iPinYou [18] and KDD2012[9]). Log transform of continuous features was conducted with no additional data pruning (rare values etc.) (as is done in our system)[10]. For each of the four benchmark data sets we considered minimal preprocessing as done in related work [12]. For each data set, we consider only *single*

[7] https://www.kaggle.com/c/criteo-display-ad-challenge.
[8] https://www.kaggle.com/c/avazu-ctr-prediction/data.
[9] https://www.kaggle.com/c/kddcup2012-track2.
[10] Such minimal pre-processing is within reach of a regular production.

pass learning, as this type of training is the most reflective of actual production performance discussed in the following sections. Batch size considered was 2500, for each algorithm-data set pair, we varied learning rate (range from 0.0001 to 0.01), Adam's "beta one" parameter (range 0.0 to 0.9) and embedding dimension (from 8 to 16). For increased readability, we report best-performing configurations for data set-algorithm pairs. Evaluation is conducted by computing metrics of interest in time windows of 20,000 instances. Each experiment was repeated 3 times to ensure consistency (seed level, single pass)[11]. The hashing part is intentionally done with an internal hashing engine (same is used in production), where murmur3 hash function is considered.

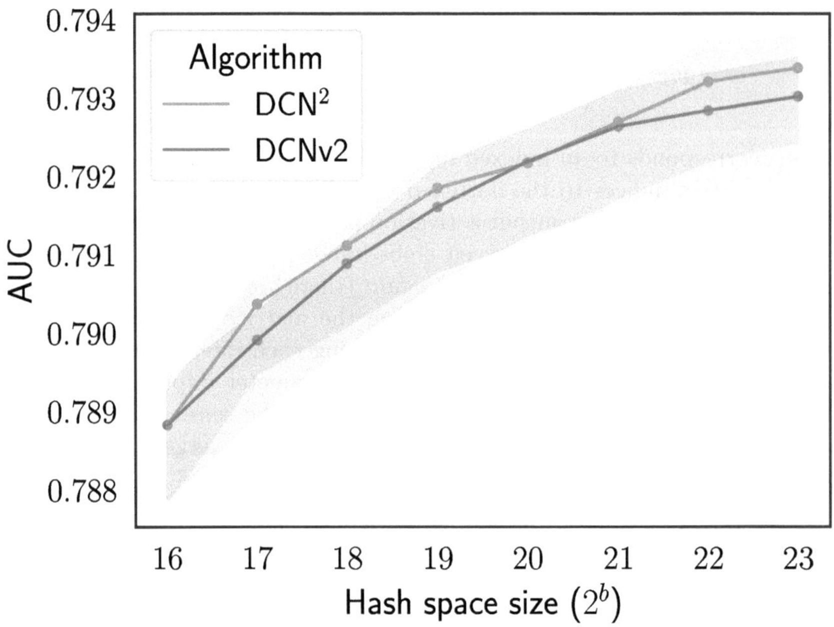

Fig. 3. Expected AUC behavior (20k windows of instances) with regards to size of the hash space (Criteo).

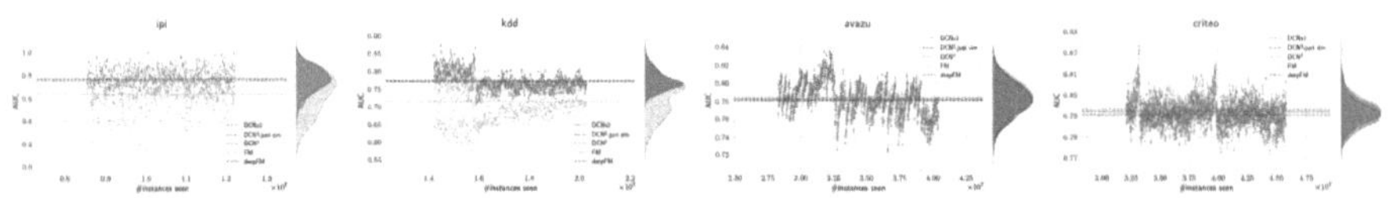

(a) iPinYou (b) KDD2012 (c) Avazu (d) Criteo

Fig. 4. Visualization of overall performance of different algorithms (single-pass) across different benchmark data sets. Kernel estimates at the rightmost part of each visualization denote expected performance across the whole data stream snapshot.

[11] Averages are also done at window level to obtain the reported results.

Overview of AUC-based performance is shown in Table 1. It can be observed that on average, DCN^2 is competitive to DCNv2 counterpart. The result indicates that DCN^2 can achieve superior performance to DCNv2 with approximately similar amount of hyperparameter optimization (budget for AutoML search was fixed to one hour per algorithm).

We next present incremental learning traces of main algorithms. Trace-level analysis is useful to better understand convergence properties and overall variability of performance metrics during the whole learning lifetime. Visualization of the performance traces for all data sets and algorithms of interest, is shown in Fig. 4. It can be observed that the proposed DCN^2 consistently out-performs the baseline approach (also confirmed by the drift of the fitted gaussian at the rightmost part of the image). Results indicate that either DCN^2 or the similarity kernel-only (*-simk*) version of the architecture offer competitive performance. It can also be observed that performance of approaches is different for the iPinYou data set, which most likely points at different data regime for this problem.

5 Hash Space Scaling Laws

To understand the hypothesized (and measured) positive impact of collision-weighted lookups, we conducted additional ablation study, where we computed models for a range of hash spaces of different sizes, with the goal of identifying possible consistent properties of the performance (e.g., RIG) metric w.r.t. size of the space. For this experiment, we varied hash space size of the best (on average) performing configurations of the models. Overview of the experiment is shown in Fig. 3. It can be observed that the DCN^2 architecture almost consistently out-performs the DCNv2 baseline. Further, the relation between the RIG and hash space size is of quasi-linear nature, indicating that with smaller hash space, performance drops for all approaches, even though less for collision-weighted lookups; this result denotes architecture's behavior with regards to different collision rates (the only thing that changes with varying hash space size). Even though collision-weighted lookups are presented as intrinsic part of DCN^2, they are agnostic to down-stream architecture, and can be used with any lookup-based approach.

We proceed by discussing the **distribution of collision weight space**. In this paper we posit that collision weights change during training (from initial value of 1.0). It's likely there are not many collision-points that would require considerable modification, yet to further study this phenomenon, we computed distribution of collision weights after training a DCN^2 model on the KDD data set. It can be observed that most of the modified weights are down-scaled (value smaller than one), indicating the network learns to silence only selected lookups. There is a distinct heavy-tailed distribution governing this effect – only a few lookups are substantially down-scaled, most are only partially modified (if at all). The distribution of the resulting weights is shown in Fig. 5. With smaller hash space, more smaller weights are observed (averages denoted with dotted lines).

6 DCN^2 Online: 0.5 Billion+ Predictions per Second and A/B Results

The presented DCN^2 is used for multiple use cases, ranging from conversion rate prediction to click-through rate prediction. It has been scaled to a point it produces more than 0.5 billon predictions per second, and has been extensively A/B tested. This section focuses on online performance - i.e. behavior of the whole system that depends on DCN^2 for inference. KPI-wise, we considered offline and online lifts – offline metrics of interest are relative information gain (RIG), and online are Revenue per Session and mille (RPS/RPM), gross revenue, CPA and conversion ratio (see footnote 11 for details). On both ends, the DCN^2

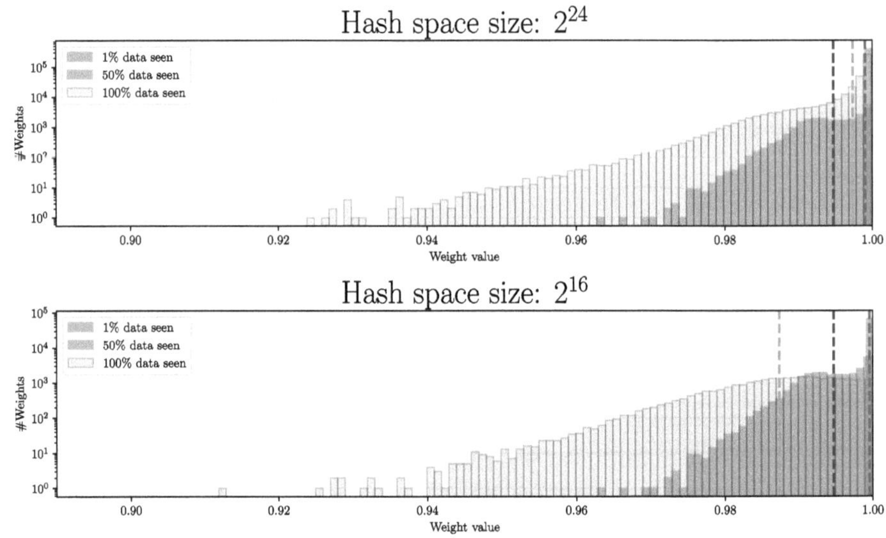

Fig. 5. Distribution of collision weights after a single pass on the KDD2012 data set.

has substantially outperformed existing DCNv2-based system/implementation. End-to-end evaluation is shown next[12].

Use case	Lift Offline (AutoML)	Lift Online (A/B)
CTR	0.0035 (RIG)	3.2% RPM
CVR	0.0010 (RIG)	4.2% swCR, 0.37% GR

To achieve the mentioned scale, we optimized multi-value feature integration through three enhancements: Summation-Based Embedding Aggregation condenses variable-length multivalue inputs into fixed-size embeddings using summation, balancing expressiveness and computational efficiency. Fixed-Length Tensors with Padding not only introduce uniformity for batch processing and vectorized operations by padding feature values to set lengths but also boost throughput, though careful padding length choice is necessary to maintain model fidelity. Data-Driven Padding Optimization automates padding length decisions via a streaming statistics estimator, using historical training data to derive padding length from empirical feature cardinality distributions, ensuring adaptability to evolving data without manual intervention.

7 Migrating from DCNv2 - An AutoML Case Study for Win Probability Models

In this section, we present a possible approach to migrating an existing model from DCNv2 to DCN^2 by discussing our AutoML case study for win probability models. Here, we refer to the AutoML as the automated process for architecture search, hyper-parameter optimization (HPO) and feature selection w.r.t. the target performance metric (RIG) in an offline mode. Beyond the change in architecture, there are two other significant novelties in the migrated model. That is, the embedding dimension increased from 6 in DCNv2 to 16 in DCN^2, and, unlike the initial model, the proposed model does not include any feature combinations—we avoided those on purpose to demonstrate the effectiveness of the onlydense layer. Introducing these improvements resulted in significant offline lift of 0.01552 (RIG).

8 DCN^2 Inference - Lessons and Battle Scars

Our production pipeline was progressively re-engineered to deliver >0.5 billion DCN^2 predictions per second while sustaining strict latency budgets. Model

[12] Result shows aggregate lift of many A/B tests conducted as part of rolling out the architecture. swCR = spend-weighted conversion ratio and GR = Gross revenue. swCR is the ratio of the number of conversions in the variant to the number in the control. A ratio > 1 indicates improved conversion volume. For CVR test, we also observed −2.8% CPA, the ratio of the Cost per Action (CPA) under the variant to the CPA under the control. A CPA ratio < 1 indicates improved cost efficiency.

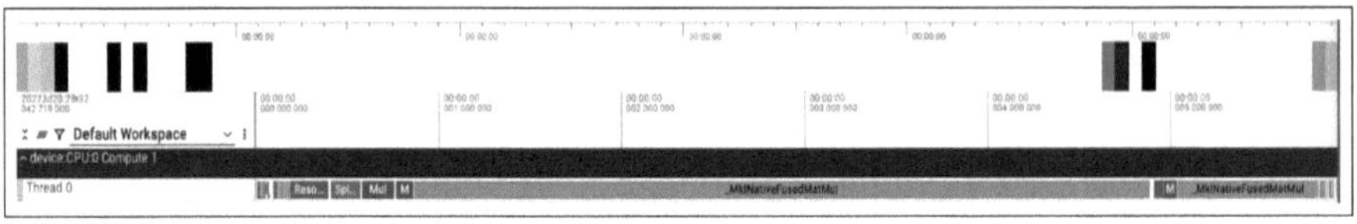

Fig. 6. Inspecting introduced layers (pink) during inference. (Color figure online)

inference first ran in a proprietary FwumiousWabbit service [12]. To benefit from an industry-standard ecosystem we ported the model to TensorFlow, then temporarily to ONNX, whose runtime initially offered lower p99 latency at equal CPU cost. Subsequent kernel-level and graph optimizations allowed the TensorFlow path to match ONNX, so the final deployment now supports either backend. Custom TensorFlow and ONNX builds linked against OpenBLAS and Intel MKL were benchmarked on production hardware; none outperformed the stock binaries, so default builds were retained. Batching strategy A "local fan-out" algorithm replaces conventional dynamic batching. Each large request is partitioned into fixed-size micro-batches that share pre-allocated input tensors, eliminating per-request buffer creation. The scheme minimizes allocator traffic while keeping CPU/prediction within 3% of the theoretical optimum.

Threading TensorFlow intra-op and inter-op threads were pinned to the actively used cores, and the runtime's background spin-wait was disabled. Removing this surplus parallelism cut scheduler contention and reduced p99 latency by 18%. All nonessential computations were moved off the critical path and executed asynchronously via lightweight queues. Memory traffic was further reduced by reusing feature and output buffers across calls; Jemalloc replaced the default allocator to curtail fragmentation and GC overhead. Combined, these service-layer changes improved throughput by 1.6× while holding tail-latency constant. Figure 6 illustrates the final fused operator profile obtained from online instrumentation.

Through a relentless focus on optimizations across multiple layers, we successfully achieved the scale, stability, and performance required for a production-grade system. These iterative enhancements enabled us to meet the challenge of processing more than 0.5 billion predictions per second, all while upholding strict latency requirements and maintaining peak operational efficiency.

9 Conclusions

DCN^2 consistently outperforms baseline recommenders both offline (e.g., higher AUC on Criteo and Avazu) and online (RPM gains in production). Its collision-weighted look-ups mitigate feature collisions in high-dimensional sparse data, yielding richer embeddings and better predictions. The lightweight *onlydense* layer replaces costly explicit crosses with an explicit interaction term, improving accuracy at lower compute cost. In production DCN^2 drives measurable revenue lift and sustains $>5 \times 10^8$ pps while running on standard ML stacks. Further, the models produced from scratch by using DCN^2 contain minimal number of explicit (hashed) interactions, substantially simplifying the final production-ready models. Future work includes investigation of more aggressive collision weight schemes and LoRA based fine-tuning of existing models (with implications for transfer learning).

References

1. Abadi, M., et al.: TensorFlow: large-scale machine learning on heterogeneous systems (2015). https://www.tensorflow.org/
2. Blondel, M., Fujino, A., Ueda, N., Ishihata, M.: Higher-order factorization machines. Adv. Neural Inf. Process. Syst. **29** (2016)
3. Fan, W.: Recommender systems in the era of large language models (LLMs). IEEE Trans. Knowl. Data Eng. 1–20 (2024)
4. Freksen, C.B., Kamma, L., Green Larsen, K.: Fully understanding the hashing trick. Adv. Neural Inf. Process. Syst. **31** (2018)
5. Ghaemmaghami, B., et al.: Learning to collide: recommendation system model compression with learned hash functions. arXiv preprint arXiv:2203.15837 (2022)
6. Juan, Y., Zhuang, Y., Chin, W.S., Lin, C.J.: Field-aware factorization machines for CTR prediction. In: Proceedings of the 10th ACM Conference on Recommender Systems, pp. 43–50 (2016)
7. Li, S., et al.: Embedding compression in recommender systems: a survey. ACM Comput. Surv. **56**(5), 1–21 (2024)
8. Liu, Z., et al.: Monolith: real time recommendation system with collisionless embedding table. arXiv preprint arXiv:2209.07663 (2022)
9. Pan, J., et al.: Field-weighted factorization machines for click-through rate prediction in display advertising. In: Proceedings of the 2018 World Wide Web Conference, WWW 2018, pp. 1349–1357. International World Wide Web Conferences Steering Committee, Republic and Canton of Geneva, CHE (2018). https://doi.org/10.1145/3178876.3186040
10. Rendle, S.: Factorization machines. In: 2010 IEEE International Conference on Data Mining, pp. 995–1000. IEEE (2010)
11. Scherlis, A., Sachan, K., Jermyn, A.S., Benton, J., Shlegeris, B.: Polysemanticity and capacity in neural networks. arXiv preprint arXiv:2210.01892 (2022)
12. Škrlj, B., et al.: A bag of tricks for scaling CPU-based deep FFMs to more than 300m predictions per second. arXiv preprint arXiv:2407.10115 (2024)
13. Song, W., et al.: Autoint: automatic feature interaction learning via self-attentive neural networks. In: Proceedings of the 28th ACM International Conference on Information and Knowledge Management, pp. 1161–1170 (2019)
14. Wang, R., Fu, B., Fu, G., Wang, M.: Deep & cross network for ad click predictions. In: Proceedings of the ADKDD 2017, pp. 1–7 (2017)
15. Wang, R., et al.: DCN V2: improved deep amp; cross network and practical lessons for web-scale learning to rank systems. In: Proceedings of the Web Conference 2021, WWW 2021. ACM (2021). https://doi.org/10.1145/3442381.3450078
16. Wu, S., Li, Z., Su, Y., Cui, Z., Zhang, X., Wang, L.: Graphfm: graph factorization machines for feature interaction modelling. Mach. Intell. Res. 1–15 (2025)
17. Yi, J., Chen, Y., Li, J., Sett, S., Yan, T.W.: Predictive model performance: offline and online evaluations. In: Proceedings of the 19th ACM SIGKDD International Conference on Knowledge Discovery and Data Mining, pp. 1294–1302 (2013)

18. Zhang, W., Yuan, S., Wang, J., Shen, X.: Real-time bidding benchmarking with ipinyou dataset. arXiv preprint arXiv:1407.7073 (2014)
19. Zheng, C., et al.: Enhancing embedding representation stability in recommendation systems with semantic id. arXiv preprint arXiv:2504.02137 (2025)

Click A, Buy B: Rethinking Conversion Attribution in E-Commerce Recommendations

Xiangyu Zeng(✉), Amit Jaspal, Bin Liu, Goutham Panneeru, Kevin Huang, Nicolas Bievre, Mohit Jaggi, Prathap Maniraju, and Ankur Jain

Meta Platforms, Inc., Menlo Park, CA, USA
{xiangyuzeng,ajaspal,binliubinliu,gpanneeru,kevh,nbievre, mohitjaggi,prathampm,ankurjain}@meta.com

Abstract. User journeys in e-commerce routinely violate the one-to-one assumption that a clicked item on an advertising platform is the same item later purchased on the merchant's website/app. For significant number of converting sessions on our platform, users click on a product A but buy a product B - the Click A, Buy B (CABB) phenomenon. Training recommendation models on raw click-conversion pairs therefore rewards items that merely correlate with purchases, leading to biased learning and suboptimal conversion rates. We re-frame conversion prediction as a multitask problem with separate heads for Click A → Buy A (CABA) and Click A → Buy B (CABB). To isolate informative CABA conversions from unrelated CABB conversions, we introduce a taxonomy-aware collaborative filtering weighting scheme where each product is first mapped to a leaf node in a product taxonomy, and a category-to-category similarity matrix is learned from large-scale co-engagement logs. This weighting amplifies pairs that reflect genuine substitutable or complementary relations while down-weighting coincidental cross-category purchases. Offline evaluation on e-commerce sessions reduces normalized entropy by 13.9% versus a last click attribution baseline. An online A/B test on live traffic shows +0.25% gains in the primary business metric.

Keywords: E-commerce recommendation · Multi-touch attribution · Multitask learning · Collaborative filtering

1 Introduction

In e-commerce recommendation systems, a common assumption is that if a user clicks on a product on an advertising platform and later converts i.e. makes a purchase on the merchant's website/app, then that conversion is attributed to that same clicked product. However, user behavior often violates this assumption. A user may click on a product A but eventually purchase a different a product B – a scenario we refer to as the Click A, Buy B (CABB) problem (Fig. 1). These CABB scenarios are not rare in sessions where users have multiple shopping intents and advertisers' catalogs have very large volumes of items. In fact,

A. Bagherjeiran et al. (Eds.): AdKDD 2025, CCIS 2796, pp. 113–124, 2026.
https://doi.org/10.1007/978-3-032-16358-5_9

on our platform we find that a significant number of conversions exhibit the CABB phenomenon. Naively combining CABA and CABB conversions while building conversion models can lead to suboptimal predictions. If a model is trained assuming all conversions happen on the last clicked item, it will learn to overvalue a subset of highly popular and click-inducing products. As noted in prior work on attribution [8], giving all credit to the last touched item or event can introduce a bias towards rewarding clicks that are simply correlated with conversions, but that might not be causing them. Further naively modeling CABB conversions impacts user experience as well. A recommender system that does not account for CABB may stop showing certain helpful reference items, reducing the diversity of recommendations. Users might then miss out on discovering products that could be useful. In summary, the CABB problem leads to biased learning and suboptimal recommendations. To address these issues, we propose a novel approach that re-frames recommendation conversion prediction as a multitask learning problem encompassing both direct and cross-item conversions. By explicitly modeling CABB events, we aim to de-bias the learning process and capture true user intent. Our method leverages similarity between products to discern when a click on A that led to purchase of B was likely a purposeful substitution (e.g. A and B are similar items) or versus a complete switch of intent.

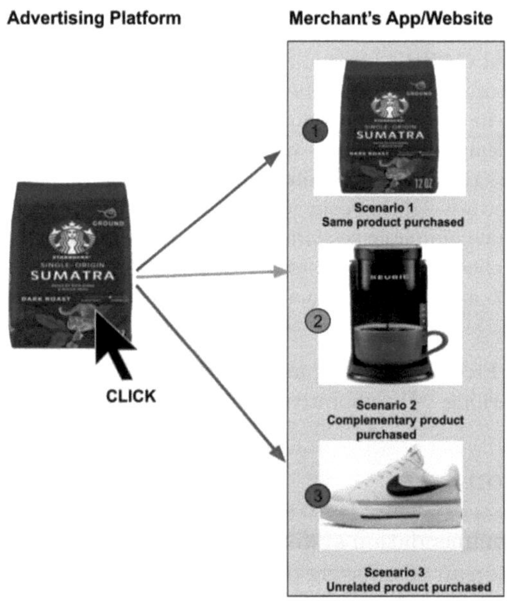

Fig. 1. Showing three different post-click purchase scenarios, Scenario 1 (green) – the same product is purchased (Click A → Buy A, CABA); Scenario 2 (orange) – a complementary product is purchased (meaningful CABB); and Scenario 3 (red) – an unrelated product purchased (noisy CABB). (Color figure online)

2 Related Works

Early multi-touch attribution work paved the way for model-based conversion attribution instead of heuristic rules like last click. Shao and Li [8] pioneered this direction with a logistic regression-based model that learns each channel's contribution from data. By employing a bagged logistic regression ensemble, their method achieved stable attribution estimates for each advertising channel while maintaining predictive accuracy. Building on such foundations, more complex machine learning models have been applied. Deep sequence models (RNNs, Transformers) allow attribution to consider the order and context of ad exposures. Several works integrate attention mechanisms to let the model learn which touchpoints are most influential for conversion [2,3]. For example, a self-attention layer can weight each interaction in a user's journey and produce a probabilistic credit assignment. Kumar et al. showed that attention-based RNN models can indeed distribute credit across multiple touches [2]. In contrast to deep sequence-based attribution models [2,3] that leverage RNN's or transformers to learn credit assignments over entire user journeys, we propose a similarity-driven reweighting approach that focuses on product relationships. Our method maps each product to a category (using a taxonomy or category overlap) and employs a collaborative filtering model at the category level to learn pairwise similarity between categories. This yields to a standalone attribution weighting mechanism: if a user clicks product A but ultimately purchases product B, the credit assigned to the A click is scaled by the similarity between A's category and B's category. Such a strategy directly addresses the "click A, buy B" problem, ensuring that related product interactions receive due credit even when the exact items differ. Unlike complex sequential neural models which attempt to capture long-range dependencies but often behave as black boxes, the similarity-based approach is inherently interpretable - the contribution of each click can be explicitly traced to category-level similarity scores. It is also lightweight to deploy, relying on precomputed taxonomy mappings and similarity matrices rather than heavy real-time sequence modeling. Moreover, by abstracting user behavior to the category level, our method is more robust to data sparsity and misalignment in long user buying journeys i.e. even when exact product sequences are infrequent or user paths are lengthy, it can still generalize attribution based on broader item affinities. Multi-Task Learning (MTL) has been widely explored in recommendation and advertising systems to jointly optimize for multiple, often correlated, objectives. General MTL frameworks [1,7] have laid the groundwork for architectures that can learn shared representations while specializing for distinct tasks. In the context of conversion modeling, a prominent line of work focuses on decomposing post-click outcomes sequentially. For example, the Entire Space Multi-Task Model (ESMM) [5] effectively estimates post-click conversion rate by modeling both click-through rate and click through conversion rate, thereby addressing data sparsity and sample selection bias. To the best of our knowledge, no prior attribution or multi-task conversion model explicitly disentangles Click A $\rightarrow$ Buy B events or learns to trust them only when the purchased item is semantically related to the clicked one.

Consequently, our CABA-CABB decomposition with taxonomy-aware similarity weighting constitutes the first end-to-end framework that directly models and de-noises cross-item conversions in large-scale e-commerce recommendations.

3 Proposed Approach

3.1 Problem Formulation as Multitask Learning

We formulate the recommendation conversion prediction as a multitask learning problem with two related objectives:

- **Task 1: CABA prediction (Click A → Buy A)**: predict the probability that a user will purchase the same product they clicked.
- **Task 2: CABB prediction (Click A → Buy B)**: predict the probability that a user's click on product A will result in a purchase of a different product B. We train a single deep neural network model with shared features and representations i.e. embedding layers but has separate output layers and loss terms for each task. Multitask learning allows shared knowledge transfer between tasks (Fig. 2). For example, signals that strongly indicate high user intent could boost both the probability of CABA and CABB, whereas signals of relative dissatisfaction e.g. quick bounce from A's page might raise CABB likelihood and lower CABA likelihood. By training on both outcomes, the model learns a nuanced understanding of post-click behavior that a single-task model would miss.

3.2 Training Data and Label Partitioning

The training data for our method is derived from e-commerce session logs, which contain sequences of user interactions (product impressions, clicks, and conversions). We construct labeled examples at the granularity of user, session, product clicked, conversion label. Each such example is associated with two binary labels:

- y_1 **(CABA label)**: 1 if the user ended up purchasing product A in that session, 0 otherwise.
- y_2 **(CABB label)**: 1 if the user purchased something in the session other than, 0 otherwise.

In many cases $y_1 = y_2 = 0$ (no conversion from that click at all) and it's possible (though relatively rare in a short session) that both could be 1 if the user bought multiple items including A and others – in our data pre-processing we treat each purchase event separately. Essentially, we partition conversion events into two buckets: same-item conversions feed the CABA task, and other-item conversions feed the CABB task. A challenge with this labeling is that the CABB category can be noisy. It treats all instances of click A, buy B $\neq$ A as equal, even though some B's might be closely related to A while others might be completely unrelated. Training a model to predict a generic "bought

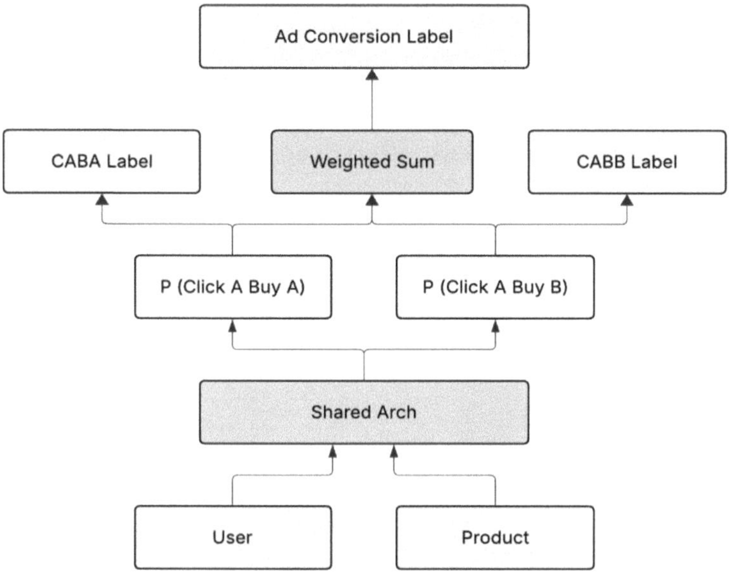

Fig. 2. Two-head multi-task conversion model.

something else" probability could be misleading and does not incentivize the model to capture users true shopping intent. To address this, we introduce a similarity measure (next section) between products and use it to weight the CABB training examples.

3.3 Category-Level Similarity via Product Taxonomy

We created a similarity metric between product ids to weight CABB training examples in the following manner:

- **Taxonomy Mapping**: Each product is mapped to its corresponding leaf node in a static, hierarchical product taxonomy (e.g., Home → Kitchen → Coffee Makers or Grocery → Beverages → Coffee Beans). Anchoring at the leaf level prevents overgeneralization, reduces sparsity by pooling engagement across many item ids that share the same fine-grained category, and preserves user intent for close-substitute items within a category.
- **Category Co-engagement Signals**: Instead of computing similarity directly between individual items, we aggregate user engagement at the leaf category level. Using session logs of user behavior (clicks, add-to-cart actions, purchases, etc.), we measure how often products from category X and category Y are co-engaged within the same sessions. For example, if many users who click on items in "Coffee Makers" also end up purchasing items in "Coffee Beans", this indicates a strong behavioral linkage between these two categories despite their different taxonomy mappings.

- **Category-to-Category Similarity Model**: To learn category-to-category similarity, we adopt a classic item-to-item collaborative-filtering formulation applied at the leaf-category level [6]. First, each category c is embedded in user space as a high dimensional vector $v_c \in \mathbb{R}^{|U|}$ whose u^{th} coordinate accumulates that user's interactions with the category:

$$(v_c)_u = \sum_{event \in \{\text{clicks, purchase, add to cart, ...}\}} w_{\text{event}} \cdot n_{\text{event}} \quad (1)$$

Event-type weights w up-weight higher-intent signals (e.g., purchases) while retaining lower-intent indicators (e.g., clicks) for additional context. Pairwise cosine similarity between these vectors yields the category-similarity matrix.

$$S(c_i, c_j) = \frac{v_{c_i} \cdot v_{c_j}}{||v_{c_i}||_2 \cdot ||v_{c_j}||_2}, \quad S(c_i, c_j) \in [0, 1] \quad (2)$$

Because the interaction counts are non-negative, cosine values naturally lie in $[0, 1]$; categories whose items are frequently co-engaged by the same users receive scores approaching 1, whereas unrelated categories trend toward 0. For any product pair (A, B), we then look up their respective leaf categories and assign the example-level weight:

$$\alpha_{AB} = S(\text{cat}(A), \text{cat}(B)) \in [0, 1] \quad (3)$$

thereby capturing both strong substitution signals within a category and meaningful cross-category complements exposed through collective user behavior.

3.4 Multi-task Loss with Category-Similarity Weighting

We embed the category-level similarity signal from Sect. 3.3 directly into the multi-task objective so that the model learns to trust Click A → Buy B (CABB) events only when the clicked and purchased products are weighted significantly by the similarity score. For a batch B of click events, the two task-specific cross-entropy losses are:

$$\mathcal{L}_{CABA} = - \sum_{(A,B) \in \mathcal{B}} y_1 \cdot \log(\hat{y}_1) + (1 - \hat{y}_1) \cdot \log(1 - \hat{y}_1) \quad (4)$$

$$\mathcal{L}_{CABA} = - \sum_{(A,B) \in \mathcal{B}} \alpha_{AB} \cdot [y_2 \cdot \log(\hat{y}_2) + (1 - \hat{y}_2) \cdot \log(1 - \hat{y}_2)] \quad (5)$$

The total multi-task objective combines the two with a tunable balance λ:

$$\mathcal{L} = \mathcal{L}_{CABA} + \lambda \cdot \mathcal{L}_{CABB} \quad (6)$$

With this formulation, the model effectively de-biases conversion attribution by grounding cross-item learning in semantic as well as engagement driven category relationship between products.

4 Offline Experiments

We conducted extensive experiments on an internal proprietary e-commerce dataset to evaluate the proposed CABB-aware multitask model. The dataset consists of user sessions from our online e-commerce advertising platform, including product impressions, clicks, and purchases for opt-in users only. We withhold specific dataset details for confidentiality but note that it is large-scale and reflective of real-world shopping behavior with abundant CABB instances. Our experimental study is designed to answer four key research questions:

- **(RQ-1) Overall Performance**: Does the multitask CABA+CABB model improve overall recommendation performance compared to a baseline that ignores the CABB issue i.e. a standard last-click conversion attribution model?
- **(RQ-2) Performance breakdown by CABA vs CABB**: Does our model improve performance of both CABA and CABB tasks?
- **(RQ-3) Effect of Embedding Choice**: How does the choice of item embedding influence the model's performance?
- **(RQ-4) Feature importance analysis**: How do CABA and CABB tasks differ with respect to important features?

We use Normalized Entropy (NE) to evaluate the ranking quality and calibration of conversion predictions. Normalized entropy is essentially the model's cross-entropy loss normalized by the entropy of the base rates. It is a standard metric in advertising and recommender evaluations for probabilistic predictions [4]; lower NE indicates better performance (with $NE = 1$ meaning the model is no better than predicting the average conversion rate, and $NE = 0$ indicating a perfect model).

4.1 RQ-1 Overall Performance

To answer RQ-1 we benchmark our final multitask model against two baselines:

1. Baseline 1 – is a classic single task conversion model which attributes all the conversions to the last clicked product
2. Baseline 2 – considers only CABA conversion data to prevent biasing the model towards unrelated conversions.

As shown in Table 1, our final model achieved significantly better overall NE than the baselines. The NE of our final model was 0.495, compared to 0.575 for the single-task Baseline-1(a 13.9% reduction, which is a substantial gain in this metric), and 0.547 for Baseline 2 which only used CABA conversions. These results validate our intuition that decoupling CABA, CABB tasks and using similarity weights to denoise CABB conversions can improve the model. Note that since our model performs better than Baseline 2, it demonstrates that using CABB data with similarity weighting adds incremental value to our final model.

Table 1. Overall NE Comparison

Test Variant	NE
Baseline 1	0.575
Baseline 2	0.547
Multi-Task Model	0.495

4.2 RQ-2 Performance Breakdown by CABA vs CABB Tasks

To understand how the multitask formulation balances same item (CABA) and cross-item (CABB) performance, we report Normalized Entropy for each task while sweeping the weighting coefficient λ in Eq. (6). As shown in Table 2, the single task last clicks attribution baseline which does not distinguish CABA and CABB conversions performs the worst on both tasks separately. Removing CABB supervision ($\lambda = 0$) improves CABA task but performs badly on CABB task. In our proposed formulation as λ increases, CABB NE improves monotonically from 0.692 to 0.505 while the performance on CABA is relatively the same showing the benefit of weighted cross-item supervision. These results validate our hypothesis: separating and properly weighting CABB events corrects attribution bias and yields a more balanced predictor than either conventional last-click training or a CABA-only model.

Table 2. Impact of CABB-loss weight λ on task-level NE

λ(CABB weight)	CABA NE	CABB NE
Baseline (Single task)	0.512	0.643
0.0	0.398	0.692
0.1	0.409	0.651
0.25	0.419	0.581
0.50	0.432	0.550
0.75 (Selected)	0.451	0.519
0.9	0.479	0.505

4.3 RQ-3 Effect of Embedding Choice

We also compared the effect of the similarity term in Eq. (3) which tells the model which Click A $\rightarrow$ Buy B events to trust. We evaluate three ways of computing the similarity weight each plugged into the same multitask model ($\lambda = 0.75$, identical architecture, data splits, and hyper-parameters) so that any performance difference is attributable solely to the weighting scheme. (1) Static = 1 ("No-Weight") assigns $\alpha_{AB} = 1$ for every click–purchase pair, treating all CABB events as equally informative and thus ignoring product relatedness. (2) similarity from *i2i* embeddings learnt from co-engagement between products which likely misses the semantic/substitutable relationship (3) Taxonomy + Collaborative Filtering ("Ours") maps each product to a leaf in the merchant's hierarchical taxonomy, then learns a category-to-category similarity matrix from large-scale co-engagement logs, enabling α_{AB} to reflect both substitutable (same-category) and complementary (cross-category) relationships grounded in real shopping behavior. As shown in Table 3, simply adding every CABB example equally ("Static = 1") injects noise: CABA NE improves significantly after de-noising the data via similarity weighting from 0.478 to 0.441. Item level *i2i* embedding similarity recover some of the gap but likely suffers from sparsity and lack of explicit semantic information. Note that because α_{AB} down-weights Click A → Buy B pairs, the model intentionally focuses on a cleaner subset of CABB events. When evaluated uniformly over all CABB instances, this yields a slight increase in CABB NE (Table 3). However, the large CABA gain indicate that discounting noisy cross-item conversions is a worthwhile trade-off. These results confirm that the way similarity is modeled critically influences how effectively the multitask framework learns from cross-item conversions. A taxonomy-grounded, engagement aware signal captures both substitution and complementarity, unlocking the full benefit of CABB supervision.

Table 3. Effect of Similarity Weighting Schemes on NE

Test Variant	CABA NE	CABB NE
Static = 1 (No-Weight)	0.478	0.552
I2I embedding similarity	0.462	0.558
Taxonomy + CF (Ours)	0.441	0.563

4.4 RQ-4 Feature Importance Analysis

To understand differences among the top ranked features for CABA and CABB tasks, we ran feature importance analysis for the top ranked features for each of these tasks respectively.

- **CABA Feature Importance**: Most of the top ranked features for CABA tasks were broadly related to personalization e.g. users' past interaction with clicked product or similar products, time gap since the user interacted with clicked product or similar products.
- **CABB Feature Importance**: Most of the top ranked features for CABB tasks were broadly related to semi-personalization (due to similarity weighting) and overall popularity e.g. advertiser historic CVR globally, users' past purchases with same/similar category products. Note that even after similarity weighting, we expect some global popularity features to show up in CABB

because similarity metrics is also trained on co-engagement data which is dominated by popular products.

Qualitative analysis of important features confirmed our intuition that CABA task is influenced much more by features targeting personalization whereas CABB task is influenced by semi personalization-based features due to the similarity weighting scheme used in re-balancing its loss.

5 Online Deployment

To validate real-world performance, we deployed our best offline model in a live A/B test on our e-commerce platform's recommendation system. The test ran for two weeks, comparing our new model against the existing production recommender (which was based on single task last-click attribution). The reported improvements in business metrics are statistically significant. The results in the online setting mirrored the offline gains, demonstrating the practical value of our approach. The treatment delivered a +0.25% lift in our primary business metric (proprietary metric correlated with the long-term health of our business). Crucially, the live experiment also showed an increase in CABA rate by 1.27% i.e. the proportion of sessions where the user's purchase was from the same initial click rose supporting the claim that our model kept recommendations more personalized and aligned with users shopping intent. From a business perspective, these improvements translate to a better user experience and potentially higher revenue. By mitigating the Click A, Buy B problem, the taxonomy-aware recommender not only avoids the pitfall of misleading recommendations but also capitalizes on genuine cross-sell opportunities (through complementary items). We continue to monitor longer-term impacts such as repeat purchase rate and customer retention, hypothesizing that the more contextually relevant recommendations will foster greater trust in the platform's suggestions over time.

6 Limitations

While the proposed taxonomy-aware co-engagement similarity weighting is central to the model's success in distinguishing meaningful CABB events, this approach introduces some limitations. Firstly, the system's efficacy is heavily dependent on the quality and granularity of the underlying product taxonomy; an outdated, poorly structured, or inappropriately granular taxonomy can hinder the accurate identification of substitutable or complementary relationships, thereby degrading the precision of the similarity weights. Secondly, although the co-engagement signals aim to highlight genuine cross-item intent, they can sometimes be noisy. Unrelated products that happen to co-occur frequently in user sessions due to general popularity or some seasonal trends might still acquire non-negligible similarity scores. This can lead to the mis-attribution of importance to some unrelated CABB events, introducing subtle noise into the learning process. Finally, the multi-task framework involves careful calibration of the loss contributions from the CABA and CABB tasks using the hyperparameter λ. Determining an optimal λ typically requires extensive empirical tuning, and the model's performance can be sensitive to this value, potentially requiring re-tuning as user behavior or product catalogs evolve.

7 Conclusion and Future Work

The prevalent "Click A, Buy B (CABB)" phenomenon in e-commerce poses a significant challenge to traditional conversion attribution models, often leading to biased learning and suboptimal recommendations. This paper introduced a novel approach to address this by re-framing conversion prediction as a multi-task learning problem, with distinct heads CABA and CABB conversions. A key contribution is our taxonomy-aware collaborative filtering weighting scheme, which aims to discern meaningful CABB events (substitutions or complements) from coincidental purchases by leveraging category-level co-engagement signals. Our offline experiments demonstrated a 13% reduction in normalized entropy compared to a last-click baseline, and our model outperformed a CABA-only baseline, underscoring the value of carefully incorporating weighted CABB signals. Crucially, online A/B testing on a large-scale e-commerce platform yielded a statistically significant +0.25% lift in our primary business metric and an increase in the CABA rate, indicating more personalized and aligned recommendations. We acknowledge that the reliance on taxonomy and coengagement for similarity scoring can be sensitive to taxonomy quality and may not perfectly filter all unrelated CABB events. To address these limitations and further enhance the model, future work could explore several avenues. Incorporating world knowledge from Large Language Models (LLMs) could provide a more robust method for labeling CABB events as related or unrelated, potentially augmenting or refining the co-engagement-based similarity scores. Furthermore, instead of a fixed hyperparameter λ, an attention mechanism could be developed to dynamically learn the optimal balance between CABA and CABB loss contributions, potentially using the final ad conversion event as a supervisory signal. Exploring such dynamic weighting, extending the attribution window beyond single sessions, and integrating richer semantic product features remain promising directions for advancing CABB-aware recommendation systems.

Acknowledgments. We would like to thank our leadership Ben Schulte, Deepak Chandra, Shyam Rajaram, Saurabh Gupta, Amey Dharwadker and David Zeng, and the Product Centric Ads team for the overall support of the project.

References

1. Bansal, T., Belanger, D., McCallum, A.: Ask the GRU: multi-task learning for deep text recommendations. In: Proceedings of the 10th ACM Conference on Recommender Systems, pp. 107–114. RecSys'16, ACM (2016). https://doi.org/10.1145/2959100.2959180

2. Bencina, J., et al.: LiDDA: data driven attribution at linkedin. arxiv (2025). https://arxiv.org/abs/2505.09861
3. Du, R., Zhong, Y., Nair, H.S., Cui, B., Shou, R.: Causally driven incremental multi touch attribution using a recurrent neural network. CoRR abs/1902.00215 (2019). http://arxiv.org/abs/1902.00215
4. He, X., et al.: Practical lessons from predicting clicks on Ads at Facebook. In: Proceedings of the Eighth International Workshop on Data Mining for Online Advertising, pp. 1–9. ADKDD'14, Association for Computing Machinery, New York, USA (2014). https://doi.org/10.1145/2648584.2648589
5. Ma, X., et al.: Entire space multi-task model: an effective approach for estimating post-click conversion rate. In: The 41st International ACM SIGIR Conference on Research and Development in Information Retrieval, pp. 1137–1140. SIGIR '18, Association for Computing Machinery, New York, USA (2018). https://doi.org/10.1145/3209978.3210104
6. Sarwar, B., Karypis, G., Konstan, J., Riedl, J.: Item-based collaborative filtering recommendation algorithms. In: Proceedings of the 10th International Conference on World Wide Web, pp. 285–295. WWW '01, Association for Computing Machinery, New York, USA (2001). https://doi.org/10.1145/371920.372071
7. Sener, O., Koltun, V.: Multi-task learning as multi-objective optimization. In: Bengio, S., Wallach, H., Larochelle, H., Grauman, K., Cesa-Bianchi, N., Garnett, R. (eds.) Advances in Neural Information Processing Systems, vol. 31. Curran Associates, Inc. (2018)
8. Shao, X., Li, L.: Data-driven multi-touch attribution models. In: Proceedings of the 17th ACM SIGKDD International Conference on Knowledge Discovery and Data Mining, pp. 258–264. KDD '11, Association for Computing Machinery, New York, USA (2011). https://doi.org/10.1145/2020408.2020453

Large Language Models for Detecting Gambling Advertisement Images to Enhance the Efficiency of the Creative Review Process

Edward L. Martis and Jayesh Santosh Asawa(✉)

Samsung Ads, Bengaluru, Karnataka, India
{e.martis,jayesh.asawa}@samsung.com, jayeshasawa1@gmail.com

Abstract. The creative review process often involves manually sifting through numerous images to identify content that violates advertising policies. The manual creative review team spends a lot of time and resources in detecting harmful content, such as gambling within image creatives. Our objective is to reduce the workload of the team with advanced ML models by classifying the images as gambling or not. For this purpose, we have evaluated CNN-based model (VGG-16), Vision Transformer model (ViT), and LLMs (LLAMA-Vision-11b and LLM2Vec encoder), along with an ensemble of these for the gambling image classification task. We are able to achieve close to 99% accuracy, with misclassification of gambling (FNR) and non-gambling (FPR) being 5% and 1%, respectively. We have also achieved an approximately 95% potential reduction in time, effort, and cost on application of our classification solution.

Keywords: SSP · Creatives · Manual Review · Gambling · LLM · Prompt Engineering

1 Introduction

Recent discussions on responsible gambling policies highlight a concerning rise in gambling disorders among adolescents, underscoring the negative effects of unrestricted access to addictive activities [6]. Protecting children and teenagers from harmful information is essential for their safety. This paper seeks to develop a method for filtering online images that contain potentially harmful content, such as gambling, and can potentially be extended to other sensitive categories. By implementing this method, it is possible to create services that safeguard adolescents while reducing their exposure to potentially dangerous content.

The manual review of creative content (e.g., ads images) frequently necessitates the examination of a substantial volume of images to identify instances of advertising policy violations. In the context of gambling advertisements, this process can be particularly challenging due to the subtle nature of some promotional materials. Additionally, manual review plays a critical role in maintaining

A. Bagherjeiran et al. (Eds.): AdKDD 2025, CCIS 2796, pp. 125–138, 2026.
https://doi.org/10.1007/978-3-032-16358-5_10

trust between brands and their audiences, as it ensures that only compliant and safe content is displayed to users, thereby preserving the brand reputation and user trust.

Our review process uses widely available third-party APIs, such as cloud vision, for initial filtering. For specialized policies like rejecting gambling content such API's doesn't perform well. Nearly, 70% of gambling images were marked safe. As a result, the creative review team has to manually classifies each and every image, which is time-consuming, costly, and prone to human error. To overcome this challenge, we investigated and applied a combination of traditional CNNs, transformer models, and LLM2Vec models to achieve better classification performance compared to the third-party API. We targeted only gambling images for the first phase, where we could reduce the manual review effort in terms of turnaround time and cost. With the use of our new system, the manual review team will be able to spend time reviewing images more effectively, allowing them to focus on the most critical cases and improving overall workflow efficiency. We do this by providing a group of images where manual review is required, as shown in the results section (Table 2).

2 Related Works

In this section, we briefly review some related works for gambling detection methods and approaches. In the domain of harmful content detection, particularly for gambling-related websites and images, several studies have contributed innovative approaches. Paper [4] investigates a visual-based approach to detect harmful gambling and pornographic websites, addressing the limitations of traditional text and URL-based methods due to rapid domain name changes. By utilizing the Bag-of-Words (BoW) model on website screenshots, the study successfully enhances classification efficiency, as demonstrated by promising experimental results on collected datasets.

Paper [2] presents an advanced approach to detect pornographic and gambling websites by integrating both visual and textual analysis. This method, known as PG-VTDM (Porn and Gambling Visual and Textual Decision Mechanism), utilizes Doc2Vec for textual feature extraction and improves the bag-of-visual-words (BoVW) technique by incorporating local spatial relationships for better visual feature representation. The system's decision mechanism employs logistic regression to fuse classification results from both text and image classifiers, achieving high accuracy metrics exceeding 99%. However, this paper focuses mainly on website detection which generally contains more than just an image, there can be text or multiple images hence it contains more information than just an image in contrast to our work. Specially the keywords within the website content helps in accuracy and other metrics a lot.

In Paper [7], the authors address the gap in harmful image recognition for gambling and drugs by introducing a comprehensive dataset encompassing images from domains like pornography, gambling, violence, and drugs. They have leveraged the CLIP (Contrastive Language-Image Pre-training) model with strongly and weakly associated prompts, achieving zero-shot learning with high accuracy and low learning costs. Specifically for the gambling use case, this approach demonstrates how vision-language models can effectively recognize harmful content, even without extensive labeled data, providing a practical solution for safeguarding children and vulnerable populations from exposure to gambling-related risks in digital environments.

Our main work builds on these studies by exploring the use of Transformers and Large Language Models (LLMs) for gambling detection and broader harmful content recognition. This approach not only integrates the strengths of visual and textual analysis but also leverages zero-shot learning to address data scarcity, particularly in niche areas like gambling detection. By doing so, we aim to enhance the robustness and adaptability of content detection systems, contributing to the evolution of detection methods in this field. To the best of author's knowledge, this is the first time exploration of application of LLM via prompt engineering in detection of gambling and potentially other harmful contents. With the boom of AI and LLM trained with such a huge amount of data, they have got smart enough to detect the harmful content and classify the images with great accuracy.

3 Methodology

3.1 Dataset

We created a specialized dataset tailored for the gambling-specific use case, derived from proprietary data logs of Samsung's Supply-Side Platform (SSP), which serves as ad inventory to various publishers. This dataset encompasses a wide array of gambling scenarios, including casino-style gambling (e.g., roulette, blackjack, slot machines), real money games (skill-based games with monetary rewards), cryptocurrency gambling (platforms utilizing digital currencies for wagering), lottery, and luck-based gambling advertisements (promotions for sweepstakes, raffles, etc.). Hence the dataset was general enough containing varieties of gambling and non-gambling images. Initially, the dataset comprised 500,000 images, collected over a defined period from our ad serving logs. Our manual review team, consisting of trained annotators, meticulously labelled each image with relevant categories such as "gambling", "games" (non-gambling related), and "cards" (playing cards in both gambling and non-gambling contexts), among other classifications to capture a comprehensive understanding of the image content. This initial labelling phase was crucial for establishing a ground truth for our classification task.

Upon initial inspection for data quality, a significant redundancy was identified, with 90% of the images being exact or near-duplicates. This high level of duplication could skew model training and evaluation, leading to overfitting and an inaccurate assessment of generalization performance. To address this, we employed a robust image hashing algorithm and a similarity threshold to identify and remove these duplicates. After this deduplication process, we were left

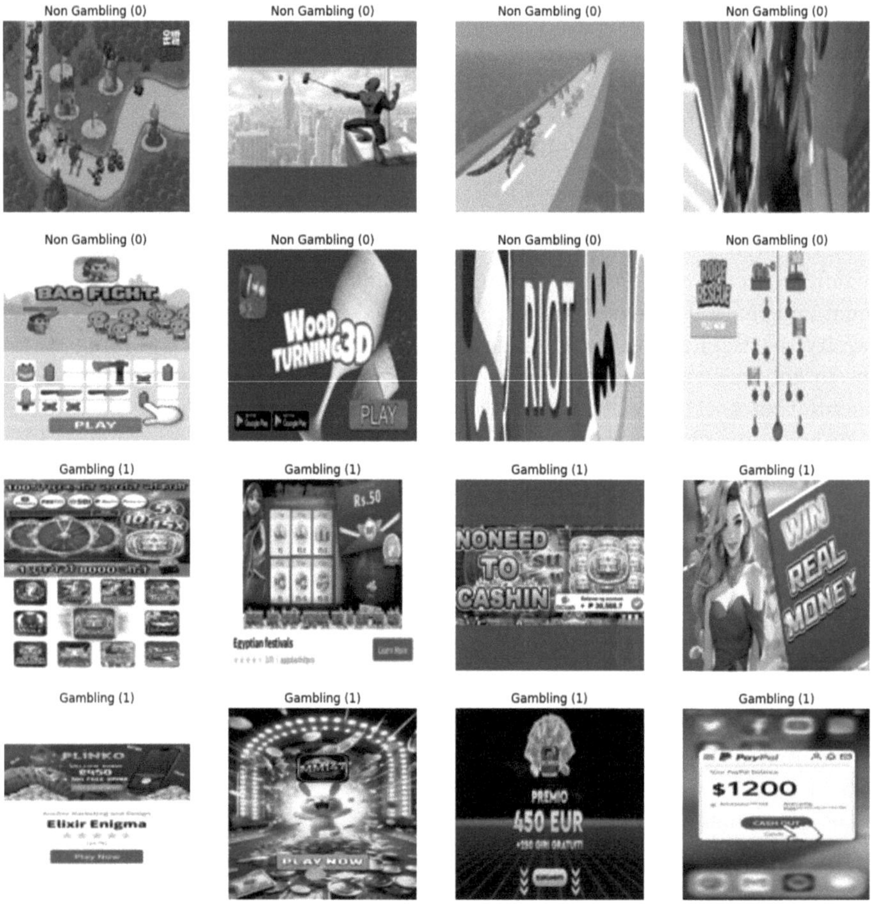

Fig. 1. Sample Creative Ads images in Dataset with Labels.

with a more representative set of 50,000 unique images, ensuring a more balanced and informative dataset. The subsequent step involved the crucial label creation process for our binary classification task (gambling vs. non-gambling). We designated images tagged with "gambling" and "cards" (when contextually indicative of gambling) as label 1 (positive class, representing gambling content) and the remaining images, which included "games" and other non-gambling related categories, as label 0 (negative class). This labelling strategy aimed to capture the core objective of identifying gambling-related visuals. Following this rigorous cleaning and labelling process, the refined dataset consisted of 30,000 images, providing a substantial volume for training our models. Notably, 4% of these images corresponded to the gambling class (label 1). Figure 1 shows the small sample of the 16 images from our dataset showcasing the images belonging to Gambling and Non-Gambling class. For evaluating the performance and generalizability of our classification models, we resized the images to standardized dimensions of 64×64 and 128×128 pixels. These resolutions were chosen as a trade-off between computational efficiency and the preservation of essential visual features. The final dataset was strategically split into training, testing, and validation sets in a 60:20:20 ratio, respectively. The training set (18,000 images) was used to learn the model parameters, the validation set (6,000 images) was used for hyperparameter tuning and early stopping during training to prevent overfitting, and the testing set (6,000 images), held out from the training process, was used for the final unbiased evaluation of the trained models' performance on unseen data.

3.2 Modeling Methods

We used a multi-pronged approach for classifying the images as gambling or not. Our strategy involves implementation of traditional CNN based model, followed by the vision transformer model, LLM based approaches and an ensemble approaches for selection of best approach in terms of performance.

Traditional CNN Model: VGG-16 [5], a deep Convolutional Neural Network (CNN) architecture, is distinguished by its significant depth, comprising 13 convolutional layers and 3 fully connected layers, totalling 16 layers with learnable weights. This increased depth compared to earlier CNN architectures allows the model to learn a hierarchy of increasingly complex visual features from raw pixel inputs. The convolutional layers employ small 3×3 filters, enabling the network to capture fine-grained details in images. Multiple stacked convolutional layers with ReLU activation functions are followed by max-pooling layers to reduce spatial dimensions and introduce translational invariance. The subsequent fully connected layers learn high-level representations of the image content, culminating in a softmax output for classification. This deep architecture endows the model with a remarkable capacity to identify intricate features from images, making it particularly suitable for complex image classification tasks. The model's demonstrated success in the ImageNet Large Scale Visual Recognition Challenge (ILSVRC) highlights its power in learning discriminative visual patterns, rendering it a strong baseline model for the challenging task of gambling image classification, where subtle visual cues can be critical.

The fact that VGG-16 is pre-trained on the massive ImageNet dataset, containing millions of diverse images spanning 1000 object categories, equips it with a robust foundation for recognizing a wide range of visual concepts. This pre-training process allows the model to learn generic image features that are transferable to other computer vision tasks. This pre-trained knowledge facilitates efficient fine-tuning for specific tasks, such as identifying gambling-related content, as the initial layers of the network have already learned useful visual representations. By leveraging transfer learning, we can adapt the pre-trained VGG-16 model to our smaller gambling dataset, achieving good performance with significantly less training data and computational resources compared to training a deep network from scratch.

In our implementation, we employed transfer learning techniques to adapt the VGG-16 model, pre-trained on ImageNet, to our specific gambling image classification task. We replaced the original classification layer of the VGG-16 model with a new fully connected layer with two output neurons, corresponding to the gambling (label 1) and non-gambling (label 0) classes, followed by a softmax activation function. The weights of the pre-trained convolutional layers were initially frozen to preserve the learned generic image features. The model was then trained using our gambling dataset with the Adam optimizer, a computationally efficient stochastic gradient descent algorithm, and a relatively small learning rate of 0.0001 to avoid destabilizing the pre-trained weights during fine-tuning. To address the significant class imbalance in our dataset, where the number of non-gambling images was much larger than gambling images, we applied class weights in a 1:40 ratio for the non-gambling (0) and gambling (1) labels, respectively. This weighting scheme assigns a higher penalty to misclassifying gambling images, forcing the model to pay more attention to the minority class. We initially trained the model for 100 epochs, monitoring the validation accuracy and loss to detect signs of overfitting. However, observations from Fig. 2, which plots the training and validation accuracy over epochs, revealed that the validation accuracy plateaued and even slightly decreased after approximately 40 epochs, indicating that further training was not leading to improved generalization and could be causing overfitting.

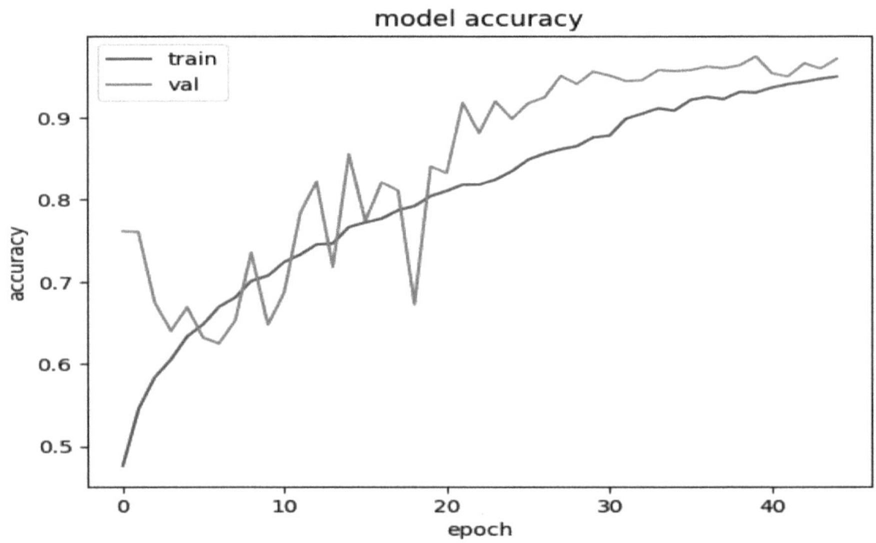

Fig. 2. Model Training for VGG-16 (with 40 epochs).

To further optimize the model and potentially improve performance, we iteratively experimented with freezing different numbers of the last few convolutional layers of the pre-trained VGG-16 model during subsequent training rounds. This allowed us to fine-tune different levels of the feature hierarchy learned by the pre-trained network. We also experimented with input image sizes of both 64×64 and 128×128 pixels to assess the impact of input resolution on model performance and computational cost. Model performance across different configurations and training strategies was rigorously compared using key evaluation metrics such as False Negative Rate (FNR), which measures the proportion of actual gambling images classified as non-gambling (a critical error in our use case), False Positive Rate (FPR), which measures the proportion of non-gambling images classified as gambling, and the F1-score, which provides a balanced measure of precision and recall on the test set, taking into account the class imbalance.

Transformer Model: The Vision Transformer (ViT) [3] model represents a significant departure from traditional Convolutional Neural Networks (CNNs) in its approach to image processing, by leveraging the self-attention mechanisms that have proven highly successful in natural language processing. Unlike CNNs, which process images through localized receptive fields and a hierarchy of convolutional layers to capture spatial hierarchies, ViT treats an input image as a sequence of visual tokens, similar to words in a sentence. To achieve this, ViT first divides an input image into a fixed number of non-overlapping patches of a specified size (e.g., 16×16 pixels). Each patch is then flattened into a linear vector and passed through a linear embedding layer to project it into a high-dimensional space. To retain positional information, which is crucial for understanding the spatial arrangement of the patches, a positional encoding is added to each embedded patch. These embedded patches, now augmented with positional information, are then fed into a standard Transformer encoder architecture, consisting of multiple layers of multi-head self-attention and multi-layer perceptrons. The self-attention mechanism allows each image patch to attend to all other patches in the sequence, enabling the model to capture global relationships and long-range dependencies across the entire image, regardless of their spatial distance. This approach allows the model to focus on important parts of the image dynamically. ViT's flexibility in processing image patches is particularly advantageous for detecting gambling-related content, where important features may vary in appearance or positioning. This capability enables the model to adapt to different visual contexts effectively.

To assess the efficacy of the Vision Transformer (ViT) model for our specific classification task, we performed transfer learning by fine-tuning a pre-trained ViT architecture using our dataset. Our initial training phase spanned 100 epochs, aiming to fully adapt the model to our data distribution. Analysis of the training and validation curves, particularly illustrated in Fig. 3, revealed a plateau in validation accuracy after approximately 20 epochs. This observation indicates that the model's capacity for generalization on unseen data did not significantly improve beyond this point, despite continued training. Potential explanations for this plateau could include overfitting to the training set or reaching the inherent limitations of the model's architecture for our specific dataset characteristics. We closely monitored key metrics, such as precision, recall, and F1-score, during training and validation to evaluate model performance. Our detailed results, presented in Table 1, demonstrate that the Vision Transformer model achieved performance metrics that were closely comparable to those obtained using the VGG16 architecture, which served as a benchmark in our study. This suggests that, while the ViT model did capture complex patterns and relationships in our data, its overall effectiveness in our context was on par with a traditional convolutional neural network architecture. This finding raises interesting considerations regarding the choice of model architecture for our particular problem and the potential need for further optimization or adjustments to the training strategy for the ViT model.

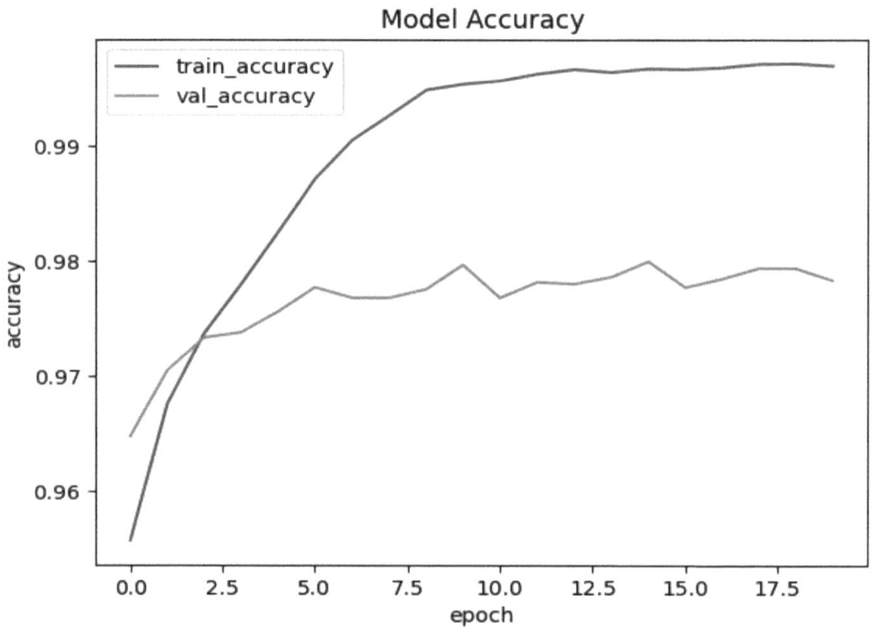

Fig. 3. Model Training for ViT (with 20 epochs).

LLM Based Approach

Approach 1: We used the LLAMA-Vision-11B model for our purpose. We created a detailed prompt using Deepseek-R1 to identify gambling related items in the image. We provided the vision model with the generated prompt and the image for classification. The LLM was prompted with an image as an input to output a structured JSON with a boolean output for gambling as 1 and not gambling as 0. We got 19.21% false positives (non-gambling classified as gambling) and 8.47%

false negatives on the validation dataset. Based on the results of this approach, for our usecase, LLMs were performing poorly at discriminative/classification tasks compared to CNN based models or transformer models (Figs. 4 and 5).

LLAMA Vision 11B Prompt:

Analyze this image and list all observable elements that could suggest it is related to risk-for-reward mechanics, monetary wagers, or casino-style activities. If absent, list elements that suggest generic advertising, entertainment, or other purposes.

Focus only on these categories:
Monetary/Financial Elements: Casino chips, coins, banknotes, piles of cash Currency symbols ($, €, ¥), "free spins" or "bonus" text Prize amounts, jackpot displays, "win" or "wager" in text

Game Mechanics: Playing cards, dice, roulette wheels, slot machines Poker tables, numbered balls (e.g., lottery), sports odds Progress bars, "level up" indicators, timer countdowns

Ad/Creative Elements (if no gambling cues): Brand logos, app store badges, celebrity endorsements Neutral graphics (e.g., landscapes, abstract art) Call-to-action text ("Download Now," "Try Free")

Rules:
Only list items verbatim (e.g., "red poker chips," "$100 bill," "slot machine animation"). No summaries (avoid phrases like "this is gambling-related"). No assumptions—only include visible/textual elements.

Example Output:
Three golden casino chips stacked
Text: "Daily Bonus: 500 Coins" Green felt table with card symbols (:spades::hearts::diamonds::clubs:)
Spin-the-wheel animation in background"

Fig. 4. LLAMA Vision 11B Prompt.

Approach 2: We used a sequence of steps to generate the propensities shown in Fig. 7. Firstly, we prompted DeepSeek-R1 to generate a prompt that would help classify gambling images. We also manually inspected the images to gather attributes that would indicate a gambling image. We passed on this information to DeepSeek-R1 as well. This helped DeepSeek-R1 to give us a further refined prompt, which would be used for the LLAMA-Vision-11B model. For the instruction prompt, which is used in the LLM2Vec technique described below, we prompted DeepSeek-R1 to generate a few gambling image examples along the lines of the manual image attribute information we collected. The instruction prompt, therefore, was a classification prompt with well-defined examples. We adopted LLM2Vec [1], a state-of-the-art unsupervised approach, to transform decoder-only language models into robust text encoders. By leveraging its parameter-efficient design and superior ability to generate contextualized text representations, LLM2Vec enables us to effectively model complex patterns in textual data, aligning with the nuanced requirements of our gambling application. We gave the image description and instruction prompt as an input to the LLM2Vec encoder. We then trained a logistic regression classifier, with saga solver and balanced class weights, on the encoded descriptions against the labels. This greatly improved the performance against Approach 1 and the earlier described models – VGG16 and ViT.

Instruction Prompt:

Classify as gambling or non-gambling. Some examples for gambling images:

Winning & Jackpot Focused:

"A euphoric gambler celebrating a massive slot machine jackpot win, coins pouring out, with a bright 'WINNER' sign flashing

and a disclaimer: 'Gambling involves risk. Play responsibly.'"

"A poker player revealing a royal flush, opponents groaning, with a pile of cash and chips pushed toward them—text overlay: 'Know when to walk away.'"

"A lottery ticket being scratched off, revealing a '$1,000,000' prize, with fine print at the bottom: 'Odds of winning vary. Bet with caution.'"

Risk & Luck-Based Imagery:

"A roulette wheel spinning, a nervous bettor watching the ball, with a casino sign in the background: 'Luck is a factor. Don't chase losses.'"

"A gambler hesitating before placing a high-stakes bet, a shadowy casino backdrop, with text: 'Risk is part of the game. Set limits.'"

"A slot machine screen displaying 'BONUS ROUND—YOU WON $500!' with a small disclaimer: 'Results are random. Play for fun, not profit.'"

"You've Already Won" or "Try Your Luck" Themes:

"A casino billboard glowing with 'TRY YOUR LUCK TODAY!' alongside images of dice, cards, and a tiny 'Terms and conditions apply.'"

"A smartphone screen showing a 'CONGRATS! YOU WON $200 CASH!' pop-up from a gambling app, with a 'Claim Prize' button and risk warning in small text."

"A gambler holding a golden ticket with 'INSTANT CASH PRIZE' stamped on it, surrounded by slot machines, and a subtle 'Gambling can be addictive.'"

"A blackjack table with a dealer smiling, pushing chips toward a player, text overlay: 'Feeling lucky? Remember—the house always has an edge.'"

Fig. 5. Instruction Prompt for LLM2Vec.

Fig. 6. Sample Gambling Image.

The response for Fig. 6 clearly highlights the "gambling elements" within the image. It detects the "Rewards", "Gold Coins", "Fortune Wheel" which is at the bottom left part. As a result, the response is classified as Gambling.

Sample Response: Based on the presence of the words "Rewards" and the wheel of fortune, the image appears to be advertising a gambling game for older aged people. The presence of gold coins at the bottom of the image adds to the suspicion that this is a gambling game for older players. The image is likely designed to entice mature players by describing the rewards they will receive after accumulating certain amounts of coins. The presence of a balloon and a gift box further reinforces this idea.

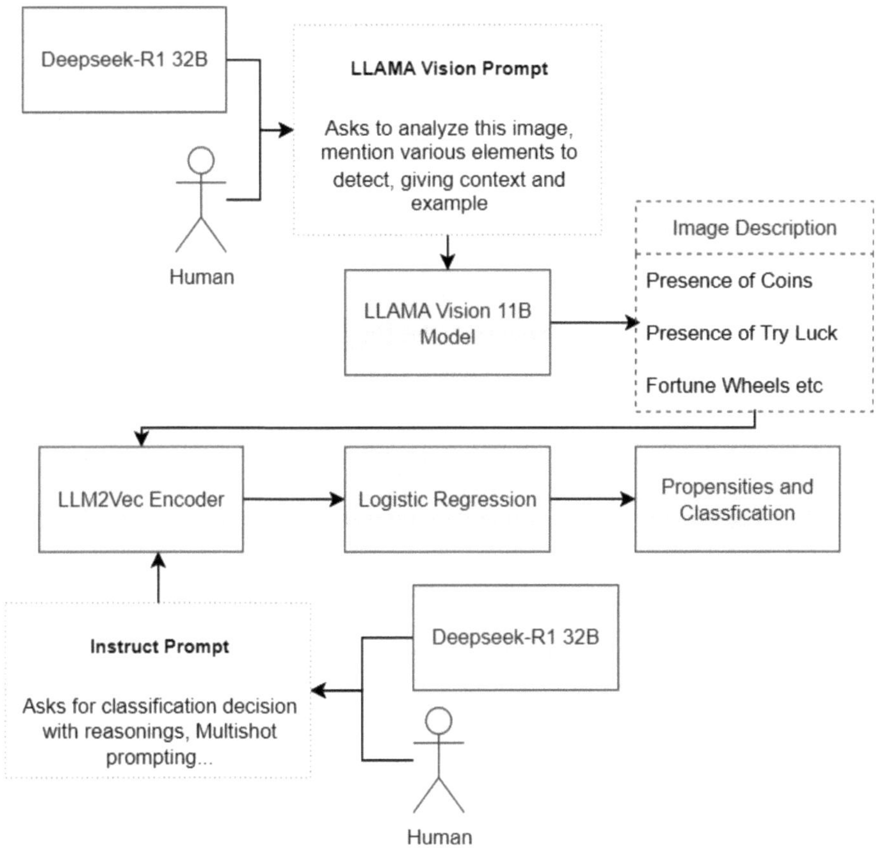

Fig. 7. Approach 2 For LLM2Vec based classification.

Ensemble Model. We combined the output propensities got from the VGG16, ViT and LLM2Vec model outputs and applied min-max normalization over the propensities and then trained a logistic regression classifier on them as shown in Fig. 8. We observe that this further improves our metrics of interest.

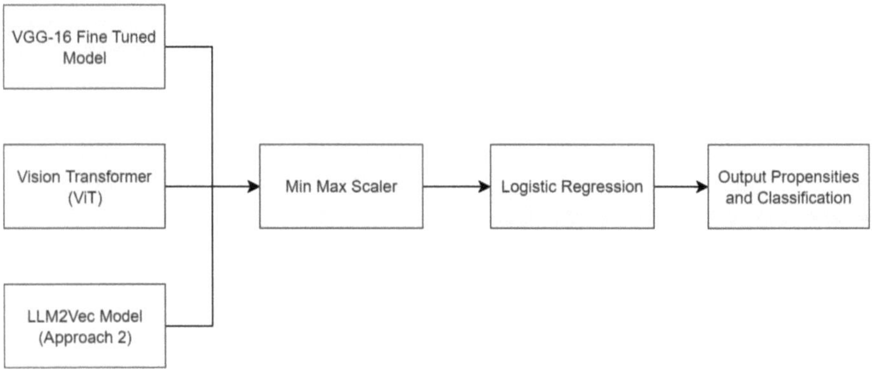

Fig. 8. Ensemble Model.

4 Results and Discussions

4.1 Evaluation Metrics

We evaluated the model performance using the following metrics:

- FNR - Corresponds to actual gambling images classified as non-gambling.

$$FNR = \frac{FN}{FN + TP}$$

- FPR - Corresponds to actual non-gambling images classified as gambling.

$$FPR = \frac{FP}{FP + TN}$$

- F1-score - Evaluate across models

$$F1 = 2 * \frac{Precision * Recall}{Precision + Recall}$$

4.2 System and Hardware Specifications

To conduct the various experiments involving LLMs, we have used the EC2 instance g5.12xlarge (4-GPUs with GPU architecture Nvidia A10g). AMI used was Deep Learning Base OSS Nvidia Driver GPU AMI (Ubuntu 22.04).

4.3 Results

The Table 1 shows the relative performance of the models. We see that the ensemble provided the best performance followed by the LLM2Vec model approach with respect to the gambling image classification problem. We applied two propensity thresholds to break the prediction into three groups as shown in

Table 2. The manual review team need not spend time on 91% of images predicted as "Not gambling" and 4% of the images predicted as "Gambling". Our model, therefore, saves 95% of the time and effort with only 5.36% of gambling images (i.e. 17 gambling misclassified out of (17+59+241=317)) and 0.61% of non-gambling images misclassified.

Table 1. Results from different models.

Model	Dataset	FPR (%)	FNR (%)	F1-Score
VGG16	Test	2.32	12.16	0.8208
	Val	2.06	12.31	0.8388
ViT	Test	3.22	12.72	0.7342
	Val	3.55	12.56	0.7148
LLM2Vec (Approach 2)	Test	1.98	11.68	0.8516
	Val	1.83	11.91	0.8414
Ensemble	Test	1.59	11.02	0.8806
	Val	1.57	10.97	0.8923

Table 2. Final Results of Validation Set with Manual Review.

Predicted Group	Actual 0	Actual 1	%age of miss	%age of total
Not Gambling	6061	17	0.61%	91%
Manual check	234	59	-	4%
Gambling	39	241	5.36%	4%

5 Conclusions and Future Work

This study demonstrates the potential of using LLMs and ensemble techniques to enhance the efficiency of the creative review process for detecting gambling advertisement images. We plan to implement models like CLIP to improve performance. We also observe that the models we implemented are not able to use financial disclaimers (generally present at the end of an image) when making the classification decision. We plan to use OCR based models to help classification in such cases.

Acknowledgments. All the work done was part of Samsung Ads. We are thankful to Samsung Ads for providing the necessary data and resources to conduct our research and experiments.

References

1. BehnamGhader, P., Adlakha, V., Mosbach, M., Bahdanau, D., Chapados, N., Reddy, S.: LLM2Vec: large language models are secretly powerful text encoders (2024). https://doi.org/10.48550/arXiv.2404.05961
2. Chen, Y., Zheng, R., Zhou, A., Liao, S., Liu, L.: Automatic detection of pornographic and gambling websites based on visual and textual content using a decision mechanism. Sensors **20**(14), 3989 (2020). https://doi.org/10.3390/s20143989
3. Dosovitskiy, A., et al.: An image is worth 16×16 words: transformers for image recognition at scale (2020). https://doi.org/10.48550/arXiv.2010.11929
4. Li, L., Gou, G., Xiong, G., Cao, Z., Li, Z.: Identifying gambling and porn websites with image recognition. In: Zeng, B., Huang, Q., El Saddik, A., Li, H., Jiang, S., Fan, X. (eds.) PCM 2017. LNCS, vol. 10736, pp. 488–497. Springer, Cham (2018). https://doi.org/10.1007/978-3-319-77383-4_48
5. Simonyan, K., Zisserman, A.: Very deep convolutional networks for large-scale image recognition (2014). https://doi.org/10.48550/arXiv.1409.1556
6. Thomas, S., van Schalkwyk, M.C.I., Daube, M., Pitt, H., MeGee, D., McKee, M.: Protecting children and young people from contemporary marketing for gambling. Health Promot. Int. **38**(1), daac194 (2023). https://doi.org/10.1093/heapro/daac194
7. Zhang, J., et al.: Zero-shot harmful image recognition based on innovative dataset construction and clip embedding. In: Proceedings of the 2023 International Conference on Information Education and Artificial Intelligence (ICIEAI '23), pp. 328–333. Association for Computing Machinery (2024). https://doi.org/10.1145/3660043.3660102

Author Index

A
Abdel Rhman, Esam 57
Asawa, Jayesh Santosh 125

B
Bagherjeiran, Abraham 42
Banks, David 15
Bievre, Nicolas 113

C
Cadonic, Chris 57
Choudhary, Ravi 1

D
Dishi, Yuval 99

E
Els, Michael 15
Engle, Abe 29

F
Friedler, Ophir 99

G
Gašperšič, Grega 99
Gligorijevic, Djordje 42

H
Huang, Kevin 113

J
Jaggi, Mohit 113
Jain, Ankur 113
Jain, Arushi 85
Jakomin, Martin 99
Jaspal, Amit 113

K
Karni, Yonatan 99
Klein, Assaf 99
Kolbin, Sergey 71, 85
Kumar, Shakti 57

L
Leng, Ling 29
Li, Liubo 1
Liu, Bin 113

M
Malgireddy, Manavender 71, 85
Maniraju, Prathap 113
Martis, Edward L. 125
Mosmer, Masoum 71, 85
Mramor, Blaž 99

N
Nguyen, Hung 42
Nguyen, Phuong Ha 42

P
Panneeru, Goutham 113
Phelps, Patrick 71, 85

R
Ramasamy, Dinesh 57
Reddy, Srihari 57
Roychowdhury, Sohini 57

S
Shen, Sheng 42
Silberstein, Natalia 99
Škrlj, Blaž 99
Stolin, Yulia 99

U
Urbančič, Jasna 99

X
Xi, Zhenke 42
Xie, Dongyue 71

A. Bagherjeiran et al. (Eds.): AdKDD 2025, CCIS 2796, pp. 139–140, 2026.
https://doi.org/10.1007/978-3-032-16358-5

Y
Yan, YaChen 1
Yang, Jiaxin 57
Yang, Xiao 29
Yin, Peifeng 29

Z
Zeng, Xiangyu 113
Zhuang, Jinfeng 29
Zimmer, Kurt 71, 85

MIX
Papier aus verantwortungsvollen Quellen
Paper from responsible sources
FSC® C105338

If you have any concerns about our products,
you can contact us on
ProductSafety@springernature.com

In case Publisher is established outside the EU,
the EU authorized representative is:
Springer Nature Customer Service Center GmbH
Europaplatz 3, 69115 Heidelberg, Germany

Printed by Libri Plureos GmbH
in Hamburg, Germany